The Last Gamble

A thriller

Bill MacIlwraith

Samuel French – London
New York – Sydney – Toronto – Hollywood

© 1990 BY BILL MACILWRAITH

1. *This play is fully protected under the Copyright Laws of the British Commonwealth of Nations, the United States of America and all countries of the Berne and Universal Copyright Conventions.*

2. *All rights, including Stage, Motion Picture, Radio, Television, Public Reading and Translation into Foreign Languages, are strictly reserved.*

3. **No part of this publication may lawfully be reproduced in ANY form or by any means—photocopying, typescript, recording (including video-recording), manuscript, electronic, mechanical, or otherwise—or be transmitted or stored in a retrieval system, without prior permission.**

4. Rights of Performance by Amateurs are controlled by SAMUEL FRENCH LTD, 52 FITZROY STREET, LONDON W1P 6JR, and they, or their authorized agents, issue licences to amateurs on payment of a fee. **It is an infringement of the Copyright to give any performance or public reading of the play before the fee has been paid and the licence issued.**

5. Licences are issued subject to the understanding that it shall be made clear in all advertising matter that the audience will witness an amateur performance; that the names of the authors of the plays shall be included on all announcements and on all programmes; and that the integrity of the author's work will be preserved.

   The Royalty Fee indicated below is subject to contract and subject to variation at the sole discretion of Samuel French Ltd.

   > Basic fee for each and every
   > performance by amateurs   Code M
   > in the British Isles

   In Theatres or Halls seating Six Hundred or more the fee will be subject to negotiation.

   In Territories Overseas the fee quoted above may not apply. A fee will be quoted on application to our local authorized agent, or if there is no such agent, on application to Samuel French Ltd, London.

6. The Professional Rights in this play are controlled by FELIX DE WOLFE, Manfield House, 376/378 The Strand, London WC2R 0LR.

The publication of this play does not imply that it is necessarily available for performance by amateurs or professionals, either in the British Isles or Overseas. Amateurs and professionals considering a production are strongly advised in their own interests to apply to the appropriate agents for consent before starting rehearsals or booking a theatre or hall.

ISBN 0 573 01821 9

THE LAST GAMBLE

First presented by Upstart and Thorndike Theatre on 23rd January, 1990, at the Thorndike Theatre, Leatherhead, Surrey, with the following cast of characters:

Peter	David Griffin
The Colonel	Reginald Marsh
Sally	Debbi Blythe
Mabel Pearson	Hazel Douglas

Directed by Charles Savage
Designed by Tim Shortall
Lighting by Paul Rowlands

CHARACTERS

The Colonel
Sally
Peter
Mabel Pearson

The action of the play takes place in property near a Sussex seaside resort—part of the living-room of Sally's and Peter's house, and part of the kitchen of the Colonel's cottage

ACT I   February, August, October

ACT II   November

Time—the present

ACT I

The stage is divided into two areas—the living-room of Sally's and Peter's house L, *and the kitchen of the Colonel's cottage* R. *An evening in February*

L *is part of the living-room of a house that was once two cottages. The old original walls and stairs, but contemporary chairs, rugs, lighting, drinks table, hi-fi, telephone. Although there are references to two staircases only one is visible on stage.* R *is the smaller area of the two and is part of a kitchen, complete with table, chairs, dresser, telephone. Upstage is the front door. There is nothing to interrupt the flow of movement from one area to the other*

When the CURTAIN *rises, the area* L *is lit. Sally is pouring drinks. She is twenty-seven and is wearing a black dress. She is pleasant, attractive, self-possessed, but with a certain vulnerability. She recently married Peter, the Colonel's son, and works in market research. As she pours a second gin and tonic* ...

The Colonel enters L, *holding a suitcase and wearing a dark coat and black tie. He is seventy-two and upright. He is a proud austere man with a hint of sadness in his eyes. He was a colonel in the Royal Electrical and Mechanical Engineers and still believes in the regulation haircut. He looks weary and feels a stranger*

Sally (*glancing round*) No, leave that in the hall. Peter will take it up to your room.

The Colonel exits

Sally finishes pouring the gin and tonic

The Colonel enters

 (*As he reappears*) Aren't you going to take your coat off?
Colonel I am cold.
Sally The central heating is on. Whisky and soda, is that right?
Colonel (*glancing about the room*) Thank you. Why are there two staircases?
Sally It was originally two cottages. One for the head gamekeeper, (*pointing off* L) and one for his assistant. (*Pouring*) Do sit down. You must be very tired.
Colonel (*remaining standing*) My legs are stiff with the journey.
Sally We could have stopped. Peter did ask you.
Colonel He wanted to get home.
Sally He would have been quite happy to stop. (*About to add the soda*) Say when.
Colonel (*waiting before speaking*) When.

Sally (*crossing with the drink*) I bet you're ready for this.
Colonel I hadn't given it a thought.
Sally Really? (*Returning to pick up her glass*) I've been thinking of nothing else.

> *Peter enters. He is the Colonel's son. He is thirty-six and not at all austere. He is a trendy solicitor and still has his boyish charm. He is wearing a dark suit and a black tie*

Peter Do sit down, Dad.
Sally He doesn't want to. His legs are stiff.
Peter We could have stopped. I did ask you.
Sally (*handing Peter a gin and tonic*) There we are, Peter.
Peter (*taking it*) Thank you, Sally. (*Crossing to sit*) Cheers, everyone.
Sally Cheers.
Peter (*after drinking*) Ah, that's better. I'm surprised Mrs Pearson didn't offer us a drink.
Sally Fair's fair. She put on a lovely buffet. She did you proud, er, (*hesitating*) Colonel.
Colonel She was very fond of my wife.
Sally I'm sure she was very fond of both of you.
Colonel Yes, but it wasn't my funeral. I hate funerals.
Peter You're not alone there, Dad.
Colonel Some people like them. I've seen it in their eyes, especially after a battle. There but for the Grace of God.
Peter Nobody thought that today.
Sally Certainly not. Everyone was very sad.
Colonel I shall miss her.
Peter So will I.
Colonel Forty-seven years.
Peter She spoiled me something rotten.
Colonel I beg your pardon?
Peter I said she spoiled me.
Colonel Yes, she spoiled you all right.
Sally (*sounding casual*) As a matter of interest, who invited Judith?
Colonel I did.
Peter She got on well with Mother.
Sally Oh, I knew she'd be at the funeral. It's just that I didn't expect to find her at Mrs Pearson's.
Colonel She had every right to be at Mabel's. She was Peter's wife.
Sally Even so, I do think someone might have warned me.
Colonel Why?
Sally I have been married to Peter for three months now. I have rights too.
Colonel It didn't occur to me. I apologize.
Sally I thought she was looking very attractive, didn't you?
Peter No, I didn't. I thought, thank God I don't have to look into those sorrowful eyes, and feel guilty at having forgotten to mow the lawn.
Colonel The girl was upset.
Peter (*disagreeing*) Well, she looked upset.

Act I

Colonel She was upset.
Peter Except I've seen that same expression if I didn't replace the toothpaste cap. Now, may we shut up about Judith? She is no longer my wife. Sally is. Let's discuss something important. Your future. What are you going to do, Dad?
Sally You can stay here for as long as you like.
Colonel I'd soon get on your nerves, Sally.
Sally That's not true.
Colonel Yes, we have no rapport.
Sally Unlike you and Judith.
Colonel (*to Peter*) She didn't like me very much, did she?
Peter No, not very much. If at all.
Colonel It was Jill people liked, Sally. Jack and Jill went up the hill, to fetch a pail of water. Jack fell down and broke his crown, and Jill came tumbling after. Only Jill went first.
Peter So you're all right, Jack.
Colonel (*ignoring Peter*) I don't believe in divorce. Never have done. (*To Peter*) Why did I say that?
Peter You're starting to wander.
Colonel (*smiling as he sits*) It's very pleasant to wander at my age. There's no pain, no tears. (*Looking at his glass*) I'm supposed to give this up, you know. A heart complaint.
Peter I didn't know there was anything wrong with your heart.
Colonel If you had, I might not have got my whisky. It's not serious. Simply *anno Domini*. And Jack came tumbling after. (*After a sip of whisky*) I don't know what the hell I'm going to do. That's what you asked, wasn't it? Jill would have known. I don't.
Sally Do you think you'll stay on at the house, Dad?
Colonel I don't know that I want you to call me Dad.
Peter (*annoyed*) So what do you want her to call you: sir?
Sally Don't, Peter. He's had a rough day.
Peter (*rising*) That's no reason to take it out on you. (*He takes his empty glass and picks up Sally's* en route *to the drinks*)
Colonel It took me a long time getting used to hearing Judith calling me Dad, and I still think of her as ... but I've just remembered, we're to shut up about Judith. Of course you must call me Dad, Sally. It came as a shock, that's all.
Peter Apropos your future, there are three options open to you.
Colonel There speaks my solicitor son. I don't know how you do it, Peter. She, whose name must not be mentioned, is given the house, and you move in to an even bigger house. It has a half-acre of land, a cottage, various outbuildings. My, my, what money there is in conveyancing.
Peter You can stay where you are and look after yourself.
Colonel Tell me, is this a free consultation?
Peter (*ignoring him*) Except it is a large house. (*He hands Sally her drink*)
Colonel I could always employ a housekeeper.
Peter (*crossing with his glass to sit*) I'd give her a month.
Colonel As long as that?

Peter You can move somewhere smaller, and still look after yourself.
Colonel I've never liked cooking.
Peter Or you can buy the cottage here, and have your evening meal with us.

The Colonel glances at Sally

Sally (*as he does so*) I was the one who suggested it.
Peter Or if you prefer, you can take the meal back to the cottage.
Sally You'll still have your independence.
Peter (*affectionately*) I'd like you to be near.
Colonel Why?
Peter In case you're ill, in case you have a fall, in case you don't eat. And you'd have company, if you wanted it. It's not as if you have any friends.
Colonel There's Mabel Pearson.
Peter She wouldn't cook for you.
Sally You'd be better off financially.
Colonel How do you know?
Peter I've already worked it out.
Colonel (*smiling*) Trust my son. Tell me more, Peter.
Peter You ought to get three hundred thousand for your house. The cottage is only worth a hundred and twenty thousand.
Colonel A hundred and twenty thousand. Are we talking in pounds or Italian lire?
Sally It's in excellent condition. It has been rewired, re-plumbed, it has central heating ——
Colonel (*interrupting*) It's not worth anything like a hundred and twenty thousand.
Sally You haven't seen inside.
Colonel I don't need to.
Peter Dad, I'm your son. It's all going to come to me in the end, so why quibble over a thousand or two? Would you rather the government got it?
Colonel Note. Already it has started. The sooner we get his money, the quicker he can be bundled into a geriatric ward.
Peter You're being ridiculous.
Colonel I've seen it happen.
Sally You haven't a very high regard for your son, have you?
Colonel I know him. He needs that hundred and twenty thousand.
Peter Look, let's forget it, shall we?
Colonel His mother was always fooled by the charm of her little cherub. On it would come, and a few hours later, out would come the cheque book. Always a loan, and never repaid.
Peter You just want a row, don't you? Well, I'm not interested.
Colonel No, what you're interested in is a loan.
Peter Why should I want a loan? Mother left me eighty thousand.
Colonel Yes, that's true.
Peter Thank you.
Colonel That means you must be in debt to the tune of two hundred thousand.
Sally He's not in debt at all.

Act I

Peter It's no use talking to him when he's in this mood. It's witch-hunt time. Why, he'd shoot his own shadow for trying to grab his wallet.
Sally Anyone would think Peter was a crook. He's a solicitor. There's no-one more respected in the county. You're being very unfair to him. He doesn't deserve it. My God, he stretched out his hand, and you promptly reject it. (*As she exits* L) I don't understand you.

Sally exits L

Colonel (*after a short silence*) Are you in trouble?
Peter You wouldn't help, even if I were.
Colonel No, I wouldn't.
Peter Well, I'm not, and never have been.
Colonel Why do liars always sound so plausible?
Peter I am not lying.
Colonel You're a compulsive liar, Peter.
Peter (*coldly*) May I remind you, this is my house, and you are here as a guest. Have the courtesy to behave like one.
Colonel I accept the reprimand.
Peter No wonder we fight. We're too alike.
Colonel You certainly know how to insult me.
Peter We are.
Colonel Not at all. I see things in black and white: you prefer a murky grey. I believe in discipline: you are self-indulgent.
Peter But I'm not selfish, I'm not insensitive, and I'm not boring.
Colonel So where are we alike?
Peter We both harbour grudges.
Colonel Ah, the dark side of the soul.
Peter And we can't forgive.
Colonel (*with a little chuckle*) I may be boring, but I'm not a pretentious little squirt.
Peter That remark of mine hurt, didn't it? Good.
Colonel I don't know why we bother having a conversation. Neither of us listens.
Peter You heard all right.
Colonel So what can't you forgive?
Peter This animosity of yours. It's unjustified.
Colonel I'd dearly love to believe that, Peter. Perhaps you will prove it to me some time.
Peter (*as they continue to hold their gaze*) When are you going to take that bloody coat off?
Colonel (*sitting*) When it's not so bloody cold.
Peter The room is like a sauna.
Colonel Not if your blood is thin.

Sally enters L

Sally I do apologize. It was very wrong of me.
Colonel (*turning to glance at her*) What was?
Sally To lose my temper with you.

Colonel It's my turn to apologize. I hadn't realized you'd lost your temper. It all sounded like sweet nothings to me. In fact, I was rather hoping you'd gone to bring in the cheese-board.
Sally You'd like some cheese?
Colonel Thank you.

After a moment's hesitation Sally exits L

The Colonel rises and massages his knee

Is she a good cook?
Peter Yes, very good.
Colonel What time do you have dinner? (*He stretches his knee*)
Peter It depends.
Colonel That sounds ominous.
Peter Usually around eight. Why?
Colonel I'm thinking of myself.
Peter Naturally.
Colonel I like a fixed routine.
Peter Sally is part of a market research team—occasionally she has to work late.
Colonel Is the cottage freehold?
Peter The lease will see us all out.
Colonel I'm not paying a hundred and twenty thousand for it.
Peter Everything is negotiable.
Colonel What about my laundry?
Peter What about your laundry?
Colonel Will she do it for me?
Peter No, she bloody well won't. She's not going to become the colonel's batman.
Colonel Will I be able to hold on to my gun licence?
Peter No problem.
Colonel What about fishing?
Peter The river's two miles away. You'll love it here.
Colonel What's in it for you, Peter?
Peter Nothing.
Colonel Now I really am suspicious.
Peter Look, why can't you accept the fact I'm simply thinking of your welfare? Any other man would be grateful.
Colonel I know. And he'd be more than happy to pay two hundred thousand, four hundred thousand for the cottage. After all, it's a listed building. It has to be. (*Singing the tune*) "It's one of the ruins that Cromwell knocked abaht a bit."
Peter (*turning away*) Forget it.
Colonel No, I shan't forget it.
Peter Yes, I don't want to discuss it any more.
Colonel But I'm interested.
Peter Too bad. You had your chance.
Colonel Another fault of yours, Peter. You always over-react.

Act I 7

Peter Just stop needling me, OK? (*He crosses to the drinks and pours himself another gin and tonic*)
Colonel (*watching him*) That'll be your third gin.

Peter takes a deep breath and continues pouring

You're not an alcoholic, are you?
Peter (*quietly*) I wouldn't give you that satisfaction.
Colonel When can I view the cottage?
Peter It's not up for sale.
Colonel Tomorrow morning?

Silence from Peter

What time?

Silence

Ten o'clock?

Silence

What's the charge, Sergeant-Major? Dumb insolence: SAH. Seven days. Next. (*Reflectively*) I liked the Army. Orders received, and orders given. You knew where you stood.
Peter I'd have hated it.
Colonel Yes, National Service wouldn't have done you any good. You'd have been more at home in the National Health Service. Patient Number five-two-two-four seven-six-five: SAH. (*He chuckles*)
Peter It didn't do Simon any good.
Colonel (*no longer chuckling*) What do you mean by that?
Peter He's not alive, is he?
Colonel Your brother proved he was a good soldier. One of the best.
Peter But he's dead.
Colonel Yes, fighting for his country.
Peter Cyprus?
Colonel It was British.
Peter And where he died is now Turkish. Such a waste.
Colonel Of course it was a waste. But that's war. Flowers die. And the weeds grow.

Sally enters with a tray

He was a brave man.
Sally Who was?
Colonel Peter's elder brother.
Sally (*placing the tray on the Colonel's lap*) Oh, the one you were very close to. Peter's told me about him. He sounded quite a guy.
Colonel As you say, quite a guy.
Peter I'm surprised every village hasn't a statue of him.
Colonel (*helping himself to a little cheese and a biscuit*) Thank you. I do like Stilton. (*Munching away*) Strange how, in the twinkling of an eye, duty, valour, pride have become dirty words. To be giggled over. By the spotty-

faced. (*Smiling at Sally*) I've been giving the cottage a little thought, Sally. It's a possibility.

Sally I know Peter would be delighted if you were to move in.

Colonel And what about you?

Sally Well, it's not as though we are going to be under the same roof. You wouldn't want that, anyway. Being so independent.

Peter But he's not independent. He's totally dependent. Always has been. On the Army, on Mother.

Colonel Peter's the independent one, Sally. Incredible chap. Pulled himself up he did. By his mother's bootlaces.

Peter I don't want you in that cottage.

Sally He does happen to be your father, Peter.

Peter I don't care.

Sally He is seventy-two. He has a heart condition.

Peter I don't want him here.

Sally You are no longer five years of age. You have responsibilities.

Peter And I thought Mother's death might bring us together.

Colonel Our deaths might.

Peter I wouldn't bet on it.

Colonel Neither would I. You'd never pay up.

Sally Shut up, the pair of you. You've just come from a funeral, and all you can do is fight. What would she think if she could hear you? (*To the Colonel*) You were an Army colonel. Were you like this to your men, to the wounded, to the enemy? (*Turning to Peter*) And you're supposed to be a solicitor. Someone who listens, advises. And yet where your father's concerned, all you can do is rant and rave. No wonder there's war. Well, even war has to end sometime. For Christ's sake end it now.

Colonel (*after a short silence*) Tell me, Sally, do you always swear?

Sally No, I don't.

Colonel I'm glad. I don't like to hear women swearing. Seems all wrong. I'm sorry, but I suddenly feel very tired. I shall have to go to bed.

Sally (*removing the tray from his lap*) Yes, well, it's been a long day. For all of us.

Peter I'll show you to your room.

Colonel (*rising*) Thank you. Good-night.

Peter (*as they slowly cross*) And you think you may be interested in the cottage?

Colonel I should like to see inside.

Peter I'll leave the key on the hall table.

Colonel How very kind. It may not appeal.

Peter It'll be your decision.

And the Colonel follows Peter and exits L

Sally waits a moment or two before putting down the tray and crossing to the hi-fi. She presses a button and the sound of a re-winding cassette is heard. She finishes her drink, places it on the tray, returns to the machine and stops the rewind. She then presses the "play" button and the voices of the Colonel and Peter are heard

Act I

Colonel's voice So where are we alike?
Peter's voice We both harbour grudges.
Colonel's voice Ah, the dark side of the soul.
Peter's voice And we can't forgive.
Colonel's voice (*with a little chuckle*) I may be boring, but I'm not a pretentious little squirt.

Sally stops the machine and switches off as . . .

Peter enters

Peter That was a clever speech of yours, Sally. It came just at the right time.
Sally You make it sound as if I didn't mean it. I did. It came from the heart.
Peter That's why it was so effective.
Sally Why did you get me to tape him?
Peter In case he agreed to give me a loan. I could have played it back to him if his memory needed jogging.
Sally Did you ask him?
Peter What do you think?
Sally So it was a waste of time.
Peter Not necessarily. I've found you can pick up nuances that didn't register during the actual conversation.
Sally I meant expecting help from him.
Peter Yes, I'm afraid Mother's death hasn't changed him. He is still President of the Scrooge Benevolent Society.

The telephone rings three times. It stops before Sally can pick up the receiver

Sally (*turning*) You know, I don't think the Colonel and I are going to quite hit it off, Peter. Or am I being too optimistic?
Peter I did warn you.
Sally Warning me was not enough. I should have been issued with protective riot-gear equipment.

Peter chuckles

Will he buy the cottage?
Peter He liked the idea of not having to cook for himself. But he won't pay a hundred and twenty thousand.
Sally But you need more than a hundred and twenty thousand.
Peter Forget the short term, Sally.
Sally Except you need the money now.
Peter No, because I'm getting eighty from Mother's estate, remember. I should be able to do it.
Sally You worry too much about your clients and their finances, Peter.
Peter I don't see why they should suffer. My God, they had to work hard enough for their money. Why shouldn't they enjoy the fruits of it?
Sally While you enjoy your ulcers.
Peter I haven't got ulcers.
Sally No, you've got me instead.

And they go into a loving clinch

(*As Peter nuzzles her neck*) You're making me hungry for bed, Peter.
Peter You're always hungry. (*As he puts his hands round her neck*) But then so am I. God, do I love that neck.

He exerts pressure and Sally breaks away

Sally Hey, steady on. (*Feeling her neck*) I don't mind your passion, but I want to live to enjoy it. (*Crossing to pick up the tray and dirty glasses*) What did you mean when you said, "Forget the short term"?
Peter I want him where I can keep an eye on him.
Sally I must say you have an imaginative way of showing it.
Peter If I'd crawled to him, he'd have been even more suspicious. He must be worth nearly half a million, Sally. Say he married again, and dropped dead on the wedding night.

Sally makes to exit L, *followed by Peter*

Sally Not a bad way to go at his age, darling.
Peter Yes, but why should Widow Twankey get it all?

They exit L

The Lights fade down L *and fade up* R

It is an afternoon in August. The Colonel is cleaning his shotgun. A dead rabbit is on the table and a dead hare is hanging from a hook. A car is heard to stop outside

The Colonel puts down the gun, quickly wipes his hands and exits upstage

Colonel (*off; obviously delighted*) Hallo there, Mabel.
Mabel (*off*) Good-afternoon, Colonel.
Colonel (*off*) Here, let me take that.
Mabel (*off*) Thank you.

The Colonel enters followed by Mabel Pearson. She is a warm, kind-hearted woman of sixty-four. Still pretty. Still a flirt. He is carrying her suitcase

Colonel Good journey?
Mabel Beautiful. You're looking younger, Colonel.
Colonel Not as young as you do, Mabel.
Mabel Is my car in the way?
Colonel We can move it later.

As Mabel takes in the room . . .

Well?
Mabel Oh, this is enchanting.
Colonel Did you see my yew trees?
Mabel Yes, I did.
Colonel Aren't they magnificent?
Mabel Quite magnificent.
Colonel I was so pleased when you said you'd come. Mind you, I don't know what they'll think in the village.
Mabel I hope they think the worst. No point in coming, otherwise. Did you tell Peter?

Act I

Colonel No.
Mabel Oh dear, what's he going to think?
Colonel I don't give a damn what he thinks.
Mabel Is the relationship between you a little more cordial these days?
Colonel (*cheerfully*) No.
Mabel Oh, I am sorry. I thought Jill's death might have brought you closer together. Pity. (*Smiling as she notices the hare*) I can see someone is going to be cooking jugged hare.
Colonel Only if you want to.
Mabel But I do. I know how much you love it.
Colonel It should be about right. I've had it hanging for ten days.
Mabel Is Peter's new wife a good cook?
Colonel The girl is an expert, Mabel. It's a joy to watch her take food from the freezer and bung it in the microwave.
Mabel Do you get on with her?
Colonel I do not like calculating women.
Mabel (*sitting; gazing at her car keys*) She is Peter's choice, Colonel.
Colonel His second choice.
Mabel I only spoke to her for a few moments at Jill's funeral, but I thought she was an improvement on his first wife. I didn't like the way Judith took me to one side and denigrated Peter. I know divorce makes people bitter, but she didn't have to tell such obvious lies. I switched off. I stopped listening. (*She puts down her keys*)
Colonel (*sitting*) You know, this is what I've been missing. Chatting to my own generation.
Mabel You shouldn't have upped and left.
Colonel I thought I ought to. I didn't want to make an ass of myself in front of you.
Mabel Was there a possibility?
Colonel Given time.
Mabel Oh, I'm sure we could have coped with it. I was quite upset. I thought you'd gone off me.
Colonel I wish I had stayed. You make these quick decisions, and then live to regret them. Do you wish I'd stayed?
Mabel You and Jill were very kind to me when I lost Graham. I'd like to have reciprocated.
Colonel Is that all?
Mabel What more do you want?
Colonel Why did you accept this invitation of mine?
Mabel I was very curious to see your cottage.
Colonel I always seem to get the wrong signals from you, Mabel.
Mabel Part of the fun, Colonel.
Colonel How's the arthritis?
Mabel I don't notice it in the summer. The heart?
Colonel Nothing wrong with it.
Mabel But you're still taking the pills?
Colonel Those are my orders. Still a busy bee?
Mabel Well, now, what do I do these days? There's the church, the garden, my French lessons, the bridge class ——

She stops as the sound of a car horn is heard

What's that?

Colonel Your car is blocking the drive.

Mabel My goodness me, I'd better move it.

Colonel Stay where you are. We're not going to be honked at. It's about time a little respect was shown to the elderly.

Mabel I am only sixty-four, Colonel.

Colonel I do apologize.

Mabel I shan't consider myself elderly until I'm ninety-seven.

Sally enters US *in a summer dress*

Sally Excuse me, Dad, but do you know whose car——(*Stopping when she sees Mrs Pearson*)

Colonel This is Mrs Pearson, Sally. You met her at the funeral.

Mabel Hallo, Sally.

Sally Hallo. Are you on holiday down here?

Mabel Yes, in a way. The Colonel very kindly invited me for the weekend.

Sally (*smiling at Dad*) You didn't tell me you'd invited a friend.

Colonel (*returning the smile*) You don't always tell me who you invite.

Sally I'm thinking of meals, Dad.

Colonel We're having jugged hare tomorrow.

Sally But there's tonight. I haven't catered for an extra person. And I am not a magician.

Colonel I don't see any problem. Just open the freezer a little wider, and take something a little bigger out.

Sally (*to Mrs Pearson*) Men, they don't understand, do they?

Colonel So we shall eat in the village.

Sally No, it's all right. Now that I know, I'll do something else.

Colonel But if it's inconvenient.

Sally It will be more inconvenient if you don't dine with us.

Colonel So why all the fuss?

Sally (*pleasantly to Mrs Pearson*) You will join us, won't you?

Mabel I always do as I'm told: don't I, Colonel?

Colonel You are the perfect guest, Mabel.

Mabel (*smiling*) The compliments are coming thick and fast today. Please don't let me interrupt, Colonel.

Sally Come for drinks first. Say seven-thirty. And now if you wouldn't mind moving your car.

Mabel (*rising*) Yes, of course.

Colonel (*as Mabel moves to exit*) Keys, Mabel.

Mabel takes them from him and exits US

Sally She seems very sweet.

Colonel She is very sweet.

Sally She obviously likes you.

Colonel It is mutual. (*He takes down the hare, picks up a knife and prepares to skin it*)

Sally (*involuntarily*) Oh, God.

Act I

The Colonel glances up as Sally crosses her arms, shivers, looks away

Colonel You must have seen the skinning of a dead animal before.
Sally I've always hated it. So barbaric.
Colonel Why? It's food.
Sally (*glancing at him*) You're not exactly starving, Dad. Admit it. You do it for the kill.
Colonel I do admit it. I'm not ashamed of it.
Sally No, because it gives you pleasure, doesn't it?
Colonel Satisfaction.
Sally (*picking up the gun and pointing it at him*) Just where is the satisfaction in picking this up and destroying a living thing?
Colonel (*staring at her*) Put that down, you stupid bitch.

A startled Sally quickly obeys

(*Furiously*) Never point a shotgun at anyone, unless you mean to use it. Never: never: never!

Sally stares at him and then turns on her heels and exits US

The Colonel remains motionless

Mabel enters

Mabel (*quietly*) Did you have to shout at her, Colonel?
Colonel She pointed the gun at me.
Mabel I don't suppose it was loaded.
Colonel It wasn't loaded when I saw part of a man's head blown off. You never point a gun at anyone unless you mean to use it.
Mabel I rather think she got the message, Colonel. Half the village did.

The Colonel glances at her, and smiles

Colonel She'll have me confined to barracks, and on frozen slops for a week.
Mabel I don't believe it for a moment.
Colonel She didn't like being shouted at, Mabel. There could be an atmosphere tonight. Would you rather not go?
Mabel You know me, Colonel. I thrive on atmosphere.
Colonel Then I shall try to make it a memorable evening for you.
Mabel You will behave.
Colonel I shall march in whistling *Colonel Bogey*. Come on, let me show you to your room.

They exit

The Lights fade down R *and fade up* L

Peter enters, studying some documents. Sally, still furious with the Colonel, follows

Peter I'm sorry, but you were in the wrong. You should never point a gun at anyone.
Sally He needn't have shouted at me.

Peter (*sitting*) He was probably scared.
Sally I hope to God he was. Serve him right. He is nothing but a thug. And he thinks he owns us. Just because he was a colonel. What was he a colonel in?
Peter The REME.
Sally What's the REME?
Peter The Royal Electrical and Mechanical Engineers.
Sally Christ, hardly the Fifth Hussars. You would think he'd want to keep quiet about it. The Royal Electrical and Mechanical Engineers.
Peter (*holding up the documents*) This is going to be worth a bob or two, Sally.
Sally What, the new city-centre scheme?
Peter It's been put out to tender. I shouldn't be telling you this.
Sally Why not?
Peter It's confidential. You see, I know who is to be given the contract. It's already been decided. I'm going to make a killing.
Sally How much is a killing?
Peter Six hundred thousand. More if I had the nerve.
Sally What about your clients?
Peter Each client will make at least a hundred per cent profit on the investment.
Sally And there is no risk involved?
Peter The only risk will be crossing the road to the bank.
Sally Imagine their faces when they hear you have doubled their capital. Except it is unethical, Peter.
Peter What is unethical about helping people to achieve a higher standard of living for themselves? I don't see it.
Sally There's no other way of getting the money?
Peter None at all.
Sally There is the house. We could take out a mortgage.
Peter I don't want any of this going through our joint account, Sally. We must keep it separate.
Sally (*wandering* US) What about Dad?
Peter He'd never cough up. He'd rather cough up blood.
Sally He may like the idea of doubling his investment.
Peter Tell him it was a tip-off, and he'd go berserk. I'd be drummed out of the cottage. It's OK to have Army Intelligence assisting you to obliterate a town and its people. Nothing wrong with that. That is war. But a business tip-off. Good God, that is totally immoral.
Sally It wouldn't appeal?
Peter The only growth industry that appeals to my father is the War Graves Commission. I know you're unhappy about it, but I am going to do what I did before. And there is no appeal. (*He crosses to join her*)
Sally But what you did before went sour on you.
Peter This can't. You wait. This will turn out to be the freshest of cream. You have my word.
Sally I wouldn't want you to go to prison, darling. I mean, what does a prison visitor wear? I don't know.

Act I

Peter (*smiling*) I shall never go to prison, Sally. I've got the old man.
Sally Peter, if you were drowning, he wouldn't throw you a lifebelt. He would toss you two sea-sickness pills.
Peter Accidents to elderly gentlemen do happen, you know.
Sally (*gazing at him and then chuckling*) You couldn't do it, Peter. You take to your bed if I have a nose bleed. (*Still amused*) Accidents happen.
Peter All right, so they don't. Still, I'm glad he's just twenty metres away. And alone.
Sally He is not alone this weekend. He has a guest staying.
Peter Who?
Sally The Widow Twankey?

They hold their gaze for a moment and then turn with welcoming smiles as ...

Mrs Pearson and the Colonel enter L

Mabel Peter.
Peter (*shaking Mabel's hand warmly and kissing her on the cheek*) How lovely to see you again, Mrs Pearson.
Sally I do apologize, Dad, for pointing that gun at you. You were right to have shouted at me. It was unforgivable. Peter was furious when I told him.
Peter What would you like to drink?
Mabel (*sitting*) Thank you, a medium sherry.
Sally He said that's how silly little accidents occur.
Colonel (*crossing* DL) Death is hardly silly.
Mabel She did apologize, Colonel. Be gracious.
Colonel It's my middle name, Mabel.
Mabel I'm cooking jugged hare, Peter. We're having it tomorrow.
Peter Jugged hare? I adore jugged hare.
Mabel I'm sure you do. It was your mother who gave me the recipe.
Peter Then it'll be wonderful.
Mabel Except I marinate it in port and brandy.
Peter Please, you're making my mouth water.
Mabel (*to the Colonel*) There will be enough for four, you know.
Colonel (*frowning*) But I was hoping it was going to be just the two of us.
Peter (*crossing with the drinks*) We accept your invitation, Dad. Very kind of you. One sherry.
Mabel (*smiling as she takes the glass*) Thank you.
Peter One whisky.
Colonel (*displeased*) I'd rather have a Campari and soda.
Peter You always drink whisky.
Colonel Not tonight. Tonight I fancy a Campari and soda.

Peter goes back to the drinks table

Sally Do you know this part of the world, Mrs Pearson?
Mabel No, I don't.
Sally We'd be pleased to show you some of the beauty spots, wouldn't we, Peter?

Peter Yes, we could make up a foursome.
Colonel (*shortly*) I've already made other arrangements for Mabel.
Sally Perhaps another time, Mrs Pearson.
Mabel I may not be invited again. Don't forget, he hasn't had any feminine company since Jill passed on. I may irritate him. At least I hope he hasn't had any feminine company. I'll be very jealous if he has.
Colonel You don't think Sally's feminine?
Mabel Of my age, dear. The age when you repeat yourself. When you forget what you did yesterday.
Peter (*holding out the glass*) Your Campari and soda.
Colonel No ice?
Peter (*holding his temper*) You never have ice in whisky.
Colonel I do in Campari and soda.

Peter goes back to the drinks table

Sally Have you known Dad long?
Mabel We go back as far as Methuselah. His wife and I went to school together, and we remained very dear friends.
Sally And yet you call him Colonel.
Mabel Old habits die hard. And he did look the part. He didn't look a Percy. Not to me.
Colonel I don't look the part any more.
Mabel (*smiling at him*) No. Now it is simply a term of endearment.
Colonel You can make it sound like a whiplash.
Mabel Only when you step out of line.
Colonel Take that man's number!
Sally (*sweetly*) The Royal Electrical and Mechanical Engineers, wasn't it, Dad?
Colonel Yes, it was.
Mabel He was twice mentioned in dispatches before being captured by the Japanese. He came home weighing less than seven stone. You're talking to a brave man, Sally.
Colonel I wasn't as brave as my son.
Peter (*handing him the glass*) You were able to stay alive, though.
Colonel I had all the luck. There was none left when it was his turn. May we change the subject, please?
Sally How long have you been widowed, Mrs Pearson?
Mabel Four years.
Sally Ever thought of getting married again?
Mabel He'd have to be someone rather special. At the moment I can do as I like, go where I like, see my friends when I like. No need to compromise. And no chance of finishing up as someone's nurse.
Colonel I'm a great believer in euthanasia. I don't want to linger. I'd rather be snuffed out like a candle.
Mabel (*pleasantly*) Don't be morbid, Colonel. We are with the young. (*To Sally*) But in his favour, you do know where you stand with him. I always say that when people criticize him.
Colonel Yes, she's always been the devil's advocate. And lost every case.

Act I

Mabel (*laughing*) That is perfectly true.
Colonel Is it to be a cold buffet tonight, Sally?
Sally No, why?
Colonel Not much seems to be happening in the kitchen department, that's all.
Sally I am waiting for the alarm to ring.
Colonel Ah, Mayday, Mayday.
Sally (*to Mabel*) I hope you like Chinese.
Mabel I love Chinese.
Colonel You hate Chinese.
Mabel Please ignore him. He's in his witty mood.
Peter Is that what it is?
Colonel Wit should appeal to you, Peter. It's always at someone else's expense.
Peter Then you must be the wittiest man alive, Dad.
Mabel (*brightly*) How is work, Peter?
Peter I'm very busy, thank you.
Sally I just wish he would spend less time on the investment side.
Mabel Investment side?
Peter Yes, I look after a few investment accounts. You know, for elderly clients who don't want the bother of it all. Apart from wills and conveyancing and the rest of the boring jobs, most solicitors handle some form of investment business.
Colonel Really?
Peter Naturally, every firm's conduct in this sphere is regulated by the Law Society.
Colonel Do you mean to say they let you handle other people's investments?
Peter Yes.
Mabel How exactly does it work?
Peter I guarantee a fixed income, and hopefully some growth.
Colonel What do you get out of it?
Peter Very little, it hardly pays for the postage. As I said earlier, most solicitors do it and probably do it a damn sight better than I do.
Sally You're being modest, darling, and I'm not letting you get away with it. Apparently, it all started when a client got so worried about his financial situation.
Peter Yes, he almost committed suicide.
Sally Peter was able to sort it all out for him.
Peter It was the least I could do.
Sally Didn't you say the poor chap couldn't stop crying?
Peter Yes, he was very grateful.
Mabel Now, that's the sort of thing I'd love someone to do for me. It *is* a worry as you get older. And they keep bringing in new legislation. I'm sure I could be much better off financially, but my bank manager is hopeless. How do you cope, Colonel?
Colonel I have a very good broker.
Mabel Yes, but *you* still have to make the decisions.
Colonel I should hope so.

Mabel Well, I just get all confused. You don't know the relief it would be if someone like Peter were to take the worry off my shoulders.
Colonel (*astonished*) You'd hand your money over to Peter?
Mabel He said he guarantees a fixed income.
Peter Paid monthly.
Mabel And he also guarantees growth.
Peter No, I'm afraid that can't be guaranteed. Although I have managed it up to now.
Colonel Say a client wants his money back.
Peter He gets it back. All he has to do is give me three months' notice.
Mabel I think it sounds heaven. Would you do it for me?
Peter (*smiling*) You're not a client, Mrs Pearson.
Mabel So I'll become a client.
Peter I'd like to, but it's simply not worth it financially.
Mabel You could always charge a little more.
Sally That's what I keep telling him, Mrs Pearson, but he won't listen to me.
Colonel We are talking about my son?
Mabel Don't belittle him in company, Colonel.
Peter As a matter of fact, I don't like charging at all.
Colonel I'm hearing things tonight I'd never have believed possible.
Mabel Give him some credit.
Colonel Never. Tomorrow he'd go bankrupt on me.
Mabel (*sharply*) It's about time you realized you have only one son living, Colonel.
Colonel (*to Sally*) There it is. That's what I was telling you about. The whiplash. I immediately shut up like a clam.
Mabel If only that were true.
Colonel (*holding out his half-filled glass of Campari and soda*) I'd like to change to whisky. I'm sure people take this for their bronchitis.
Peter You are not disabled, Dad. The bottle is over there.

The Colonel crosses to the drinks table

Sally Surely one more client wouldn't make that much difference, Peter?
Peter I'd rather not, darling.
Mabel But I do need help. And I am a friend of the family.
Peter That's why I would prefer you not to be a client, Mrs Pearson. Why, I would be mortified if there was no growth one year.
Mabel But I'd understand, Peter. Even I know the market can go down as well as up. It would be such a comfort. Not having to make decisions, not having to worry; and to know how much is coming in every month. I'd be able to budget for the first time.
Peter (*kindly*) How much capital have you, Mrs Pearson?
Mabel Oh, it must be over two hundred thousand pounds.
Peter Over two hundred thousand? And is your income from it twenty thousand plus a year?
Mabel Nothing like it.
Peter It should be.

Act I

Mabel And that would be guaranteed?
Peter I'll tell you what I'll do. I'll send you a complete breakdown.
Mabel Would you? I'd be so grateful.

The alarm is faintly heard

Colonel I think I can hear an alarm bell.
Peter I notice there's nothing wrong with your hearing, Dad.
Colonel Not when it comes to alarm bells, Peter.
Mabel When I get the breakdown, I'll show it to my bank manager and ask his opinion.
Sally (*to Mabel*) What you must do is get him to scrutinize it, and explain everything to you.
Peter Yes, of course. He may advise against it.
Sally Darling, I shall need your help in the kitchen.
Peter Of course, darling. Do excuse us.

Peter follows Sally out

Mabel You really must show him some affection, Colonel.
Colonel Hold on to your capital, Mabel.
Mabel He's all you've got.
Colonel I wouldn't want you to lose out.
Mabel Peter has always lost out.
Colonel Not when Jill was alive.
Mabel Ah, but she preferred the living to the departed.
Colonel Everyone seems to get a good Press but me.

Peter enters and stops, briefcase in hand

Mabel (*smiling*) That just proves I'm very fond of you. In spite of you. Are you receiving the right signal this time?
Colonel I hope so.
Mabel So do I. I've been very lonely since you left.
Peter (*opening his briefcase as he crosses*) You're wanted, Dad. I'm hopeless at sharpening the carving knife.
Colonel I thought we were having Chinese.
Peter Including duck.
Colonel A dead duck? (*Crossing to exit*) Good God, how barbaric.

The Colonel exits

Peter (*taking out some papers*) I have a typical investment account here, Mrs Pearson. (*Handing them to Mabel*) As you will see, it's perfectly straightforward, and so simple.
Mabel Thank you. (*Looking at the top sheet*) It takes two to start an argument, Peter.
Peter I have to defend myself, or he'd walk all over me.
Mabel I know he can be awkward, and I've said it to his face, so I'm not being disloyal.
Peter Yes, but he takes it from you.

Mabel Because he knows I appreciate his good qualities. He does have them.

Peter But I've tried with him.

Mabel Will you do me a favour?

Peter Yes, of course.

Mabel Keep trying. (*Looking again at the top sheet*) There, that's the end of the homily.

Peter (*gazing at her and with a change of tone*) You do know about his heart?

Mabel (*frowning as she glances at him*) It's not serious, is it?

Peter No, no. Heaven forbid.

Mabel You've spoken to his doctor.

Peter What, go behind Dad's back?

Mabel But you've heard something.

Peter No.

Mabel Then why mention it? After all, he's had it for some time now.

Peter I'm sure he doesn't want anyone to worry about it.

Mabel *He's* told you.

Peter Please, he's fine. He has never felt fitter.

Mabel turns to look again at the top sheet

Does it make sense to you?

Mabel (*handing him the papers*) It's no good, Peter. I didn't bring my reading glasses.

Peter Oh. It's just that with gilts falling, now's a good time to buy. What I suggest you do is ask your bank manager on Monday to sell everything ——

Mabel (*interrupting and still worried about the Colonel*) It's no use, Peter. I know you're being very kind, but I shan't remember a word. You put it in writing, as you said you would. And I thought your father was looking so well.

Peter He is well, Mrs Pearson. I was simply asking if you knew.

Mabel It was your tone of voice, Peter.

Peter I didn't mean to upset you. Thank goodness you won't remember it.

Mabel Of course I shall remember it.

Peter Well, don't say anything to Dad. He didn't want you to know.

Mabel What doesn't he want me to know?

Peter If I told you and he found out, he'd really lay into me. And you know what his temper's like. It wouldn't do that old ticker of his any good, Mrs Pearson. It wouldn't do it any good at all. Believe me.

Mabel I can't get over it. He seemed fighting fit and so enthusiastic about everything. He loves those yew trees doesn't he?

Peter Does he? He's never said. I must remember to keep them in good shape.

The Colonel enters

Colonel I'm afraid I've blotted my copybook.

Mabel Again?

Colonel (*singing*) "Again, and again, and again. When I was single, my pockets did jingle, I wish I were single again." I said to her, "Why is it etiquette to be a dead duck, but socially unacceptable to be a dead hare?" She didn't answer. Just kept slamming saucepan lids.
Mabel Peter tells me you're not as well as you were.
Peter I never said that, Mrs Pearson.
Colonel (*frowning*) He had no right to say that. It's not true. What did he tell you?
Mabel (*starting to backtrack*) He was concerned about your health, that's all.
Colonel There's nothing wrong with my health. At my last check-up, the quack said I was fitter than he was, and he's forty. (*To Peter*) What did you have to say that to Mrs Pearson for?
Mabel He was only making conversation, Colonel. It is allowed. It is his house. And I must say it has tremendous character, Peter.
Peter Would you like a guided tour?
Mabel Yes, I would.
Peter It was originally two cottages. Hence the two staircases.

Mabel follows and then turns as...

Peter exits

Mabel Aren't you coming?
Colonel Climb the stairs and I might get a heart attack. What did he say to you?
Mabel I think he loves you, Colonel.
Colonel Careful, or I will get a heart attack.
Mabel (*quietly*) Never tempt providence, Percy. Especially at your age.

Mabel exits

The Colonel picks up his glass, glances casually at the investment account, notices the papers relating to the new city-centre scheme and starts to flick through them. The click of the cassette stopping is heard, followed by the sound of the button popping out. Curious, he wanders over to the hi-fi, looks at it, bends down, presses the re-wind button, waits a few moments and then presses the stop button before pressing the play button

Mabel's voice At the moment I can do as I like, go where I like, see my friends when I like. No need to compromise. And no chance of finishing up as someone's nurse.
Colonel's voice I'm a great believer in euthanasia. I don't want to linger. I'd rather be snuffed out like a candle.

The Colonel stops the cassette and then presses the wind button

Sally (*off* L; *calling in a dulcet tone*) Dinner.

The Colonel looks a puzzled man as he slowly straightens up

The Lights fade down and then fade up to day

It is now October and the Colonel, Sally and Peter are about to play Scrabble. They each dip into the bag and select seven letters

Peter What exactly happened?
Colonel My steering failed. I crashed into a tree.
Sally You could have killed yourself.
Colonel That's what the AA chap said.
Peter You ought to have that car serviced regularly.
Colonel You borrowed it the other day. Did you notice anything wrong with the steering?
Peter Now I come to think of it, it was very slack.
Sally Do you know the cause?
Colonel The AA chap thought some pin or other could have been fractured when I had my last bang. He may not have said a pin. I can't remember.
Peter You shouldn't be allowed on the road. You're a menace.
Colonel I've been driving for fifty years. Not once have I had an endorsement.
Peter Only because all the other drivers give you a wide berth.
Sally (*putting down four letters*) Eighteen.
Colonel I don't mind telling you it shook me up a bit. I think the car's a write-off.
Peter You've only yourself to blame.
Colonel Yes.

In the silence the click of the cassette is heard as it stops and the Colonel slowly glances round at the hi-fi

Sally (*rising and crossing*) How stupid of me. I forgot to turn up the sound. (*Switching off the machine, she returns to the table and jots down her score*)
Colonel Why didn't you tell me?
Peter Tell you what?
Colonel That you weren't happy with the steering.
Peter I'm hardly used to driving your car. It didn't register at the time.
Colonel (*with a nod*) Ah.
Peter And even if I had, you wouldn't have taken any notice. Or you'd have said it was my fault.
Colonel I did.
Peter Did what?
Colonel Say it was your fault.
Peter (*frowning*) Who to?
Colonel The AA chap.
Peter (*staring*) You accused me of tampering with your car?
Colonel I said it as a joke.
Peter But you had no right to do that.
Colonel He took it as a joke.
Peter But it's the sort of thing people remember.
Colonel Does it matter?
Sally (*impatiently*) Of course it doesn't matter. It's your turn, Peter.
Peter (*irritably*) I know, I know. (*After a short silence*) What exactly did you say to him?

Act I

Sally It's not important, Peter.
Peter That I'm trying to do you in?
Sally The way you're going on about it, anyone would think you were.

Peter looks at his letters and then places three on the board

Peter Seven.

Sally jots down the score

Colonel (*studying his letters*) Mrs Pearson phoned. Said she'd sent you the cheque.
Peter The money has already been invested.
Colonel Very foolish.
Peter What is?
Colonel To hand over control of your own capital.
Sally Don't be unfair. You were here. You heard her. She pleaded with Peter to take the worry off her shoulders.
Colonel Yes, she can be very naïve.
Sally How is she?
Colonel Very concerned about me. And about my health. Do you know why, Peter?
Peter What are you accusing me of now?
Colonel Why do you keep going on the defensive? I'm not accusing you of anything. (*Putting down four letters*) Fourteen. (*Taking four letters from the bag and simply as conversation*) What's happening about that city-centre scheme?
Peter How should I know?
Colonel Well, you did have all the relevant documents.
Peter (*looking at him*) No, I didn't.
Colonel Of course you did. They were there on your briefcase, I saw them.
Peter That was private and confidential.
Colonel Nonsense. Anyone can buy a copy. I even saw it in the library. Why pretend it was private and confidential?
Peter I'd forgotten it had now been published.
Colonel So how did you get hold of your copy?
Peter One of the architects is a client.
Colonel Then you do know about it.
Peter (*trying to control his exasperation*) Of course I know about it. I just told you, I'm solicitor to one of the architects.
Colonel But you said you didn't know.
Peter I didn't know what you were talking about.
Colonel What did you think I was talking about?
Peter Why all these bloody questions?
Colonel There would only have been one if you'd bloody well answered it.
Sally Please, the pair of you are giving me a headache. Now, either you want to play Scrabble or you don't.
Colonel I don't want to play Scrabble.
Sally I don't want to play Scrabble either.
Colonel Then why the hell are we playing it?

Sally (*rising, folding her arms and trying not to lose her temper*) You're always going on about how lonely you are at weekends. How the weekends drag. How you can't wait for Monday. So I thought, now, how can I occupy his mind? I was thinking of you. I'm sorry. I promise not to do it ever again.

The phone rings and Peter answers it

Peter Yes? ... Hallo, Jimmy. (*Pause*) But surely the cheque can go via the syndicate.
Sally Shouldn't you take your call in the study, Peter?
Peter (*glancing at Sally*) What? (*Glancing at the Colonel*) Oh, yes. (*Into the receiver*) Hold on.

Sally crosses to pick up the receiver as ...

Peter exits L

Sally He'll be with you in a moment, Mr Dunsett. ... Yes, very well, thank you. ... How very kind. We shall look forward to that. Here's Peter now. (*She replaces the receiver*)
Colonel Dunsett. Isn't he a councillor?
Sally I don't honestly know.
Colonel He is.
Sally Is he?
Colonel Yes. I've seen his name in the local paper.
Sally I'm not a political animal, Dad.
Colonel But you have met him.
Sally Only to say hallo to. He's a client of Peter's.
Colonel And yet you didn't know he was a councillor?
Sally No, I didn't. I'm surprised.
Colonel Why?
Sally He doesn't seem the type. Oh, he's always very polite; but, well, he is rather rough-and-ready.
Colonel Do you know what he does?
Sally I'm not sure, but I believe he's in the building trade.
Colonel You must know whether he is or not, Sally.
Sally No, because I don't involve myself in Peter's business affairs.
Colonel Now it's my turn to be surprised. I'd have said you would have done. Why don't you?
Sally I get confused. Like Mrs Pearson.
Colonel I can't believe that, Sally.
Sally When I came into an inheritance, I didn't know where to start. It was Peter who advised me. He's a very shrewd businessman, Dad.
Colonel And what was this shrewd advice of his?
Sally (*glancing at her watch*) Shall I make you a cup of tea?
Colonel No, thank you. (*Rising a shade unsteadily*) I think I'll go and lie down. I still feel wobbly from the accident. Peter got very annoyed when he heard I had blamed him for it. Strange he should have reacted like that, don't you agree?

Sally (*sweetly*) Yes, I do, Dad. You'd think he would be used to it by now.
Colonel You're very loyal, Sally.
Sally Thank you.
Colonel It wasn't meant as a compliment.

He exits L

Sally (*as he does, taking a deep breath*) Dad, our new dining-room furniture is now arriving next Wednesday morning.
Colonel (*off*) Leave me the key. I shall see to it.
Sally I'll remind you on Tuesday.

Peter enters L

Peter And you can remind me to lock my study door. I don't want him snooping around.
Sally He kept plying me with questions about Jimmy Dunsett. I didn't know how much I should tell him: not that I know very much. He must have thought I was ga-ga the way I answered him.
Peter He would love to find out the truth. My God, would he love it.
Sally He also wanted to know what your advice to me was.
Peter Advice about what?
Sally My inheritance.
Peter Did you tell him?
Sally Of course not. It's bad enough having him shooting at us. Blowed if I'm going to start passing him the ammunition.
Peter Yes, I'd never have heard the last of it. "A kept man, Peter? A kept man? The worm has a stronger backbone than you."
Sally Was the call important?
Peter No. It was simply a question of how to offload Mrs Pearson's capital on to the market.
Sally Why, are there problems?
Peter No, no. But it has to be done with discretion.
Sally I think you ought not to use Mrs Pearson's capital. I'm serious. You're going to do very well as it is.
Peter Ah, but think of her face when she hears she has made a twenty per cent profit on her capital.
Sally Now, hold on Peter. You said your clients' capital would double itself: at least.
Peter (*smiling*) Not in the first month, Sally. I meant the first month. After it's known who is to be given the tender.
Sally When will that be?
Peter The full council meets to approve the various proposals in three weeks' time. That's when the company that's to be given the building contract will be announced. All we have to do is somehow get through the next three weeks.
Sally What if you've picked the wrong company, Peter?
Peter I have not picked the wrong company, Sally.
Sally But if you have.
Peter That's impossible.

Sally The impossible has sometimes been known to happen. What would you do?
Peter (*after a short silence*) You know, it was almost fate, wasn't it?
Sally What was?
Peter That Dad's steering should have failed today.
Sally I don't get it.
Peter It proves just how easy it is for a fatal accident to happen to someone.
Sally (*gazing at Peter*) That is sick humour, Peter.
Peter Don't you like sick humour?
Sally No.
Peter Then you won't want to hear how dear old sweet old Mrs Pearson has been fiddling the Inland Revenue.
Sally (*smiling in disbelief*) She hasn't, has she?
Peter Yes.
Sally But how?
Peter By not declaring income received in cash from a holiday cottage she owns.
Sally Naughty girl!
Peter A very naughty girl!
Sally What did she say when you pointed it out?
Peter The poor thing became hopelessly confused. Fortunately she quickly recovered her wits when I said I would do my best to cover up her naughtiness.
Sally You didn't make it out to be the crime of the century, did you?
Peter No, but I wanted her to be grateful. It now means I have a hold over her. Very important to have a hold over people. As insurance. You never know when you might have to put in a claim.
Sally So what is your hold over me?
Sally The fact we're partners in crime.
Sally Crime. What crime?
Peter (*crossing to caress her face and neck*) The crime of being in love, my beautiful.
Sally And your first wife?
Peter She voluntarily agreed to undergo psychiatric treatment, and then discharged herself. Hospitals don't like you doing that. Once they put a name-tag on you, to hell with free-will.
Sally What is your hold over your father?
Peter I don't need one because I don't need him. Well, certainly not for three weeks. And never, if I make a killing.
Sally But if you don't make a killing: what then?
Peter (*softly*) I shall make a killing Sally. Whatever happens, I shall make a killing.

CURTAIN

ACT II

Three weeks later—November. Night

When the CURTAIN *rises, the living-room* L *is lit. Sally is holding a paperback and looking at the page, but nothing is registering. Peter is hunched in a chair by the phone, his hands between his knees*

After several seconds of silence, the phone rings. He quickly answers it, watched by a tense-looking Sally

Peter (*into the receiver*) Yes? (*After a pause*) Thank you.

He replaces the receiver and Sally waits for him to speak

They have been granted the tender.

Looking completely drained, Sally lies back in her chair

Sally Oh, God. Oh, my God.
Peter (*rising and then sitting*) I can't stand. I'm shaking too much.
Sally All that waiting. God, I could never do it again. I'd rather die.
Peter To think I am now going to make at least a million.
Sally My God, Peter, this is better than an orgasm. Think of it. No-one has lost. Everyone has gained. Capitalism at its philanthropic best.
Peter Property in Bermuda. A little retreat in Switzerland. Live on half the interest, and reinvest the other half. Give up the profession, and enter politics.
Sally I'd be very good as a politician's wife. Hats make me look ethereal.
Peter Do the wives of politicians wear hats?
Sally They do when they glance down a coal-mine. Or wave as they pass an oil-rig. God, you would think we'd want to celebrate, open a bottle of bubbly, make passionate love, drive into the night.
Peter (*hands behind his head*) I just want to sit and bask in the beauty of it all.
Sally So do I.
Peter No-one can ever turn round again and say I've no guts.
Sally No-one will know, darling.
Peter That is true. But it doesn't matter. I know. And that's enough.
Sally (*stretching herself and gazing at the wall opposite*) Let's do something crazy on Saturday. Morning coffee in Paris. Afternoon tea in Geneva. Dinner in Roma. I haven't had my bottom pinched in yonks. Yes, dinner in Roma.
Peter No, not until the shares go through the roof. Remember, we're having to pay certain monthly incomes out of our own pocket.

Sally Oh dear. Your father's still not safe from a grizzly end. I know how I'm going to do it.

Peter How?

Sally I'm going to bore him to death with holidays I've captured on my video camera. Death by a thousand yawns. Peter, what is that?

Peter What is what?

Sally Over there. By the fireplace.

Peter (*idly glancing across*) You mean the old push-button to summon the servants?

Sally (*crossing to investigate*) It's new.

Peter It has always been there.

Sally It doesn't look like the same fitting. It has perforations.

Peter (*crossing to investigate*) Where?

Sally Shall I get a torch?

Peter taps the outer casing and static is heard

Sally What's that noise?

Peter Static. It's live.

Sally But it doesn't make sense. What is it?

Peter I don't know.

Sally Tap it again.

Peter taps. But this time there is no sound

Peter It's dead now. (*He unscrews the outer casing*)

Sally This is scarey, Peter. Just what is going on?

Peter feels inside the gap and pulls out a long thin tubular microphone

Peter A microphone.

Sally A microphone?

Peter gives a sudden yank and that is sufficient to cut the flex

Peter (*handing the microphone to Sally*) Here. (*He screws back the outer casing*)

Sally Are we going mad? What does it mean?

Peter It means we were being bugged. Someone was bugging us.

Sally But who would do such a thing? Your father. It has to be your father.

Peter Yes, it can only be Dad.

Sally Just who the hell does he think he is?

Peter The point is, have we given anything away? Because if we have, he could get on to the Law Society. Tell them I've been using my clients' money for personal gain. Would he do that? Or would he confront me with it first? How much does he know?

Sally Let's go and find out.

Peter Very well. But remember. We're only angry with him because he has been bugging us.

Sally That man has been bugging me since I first met him. Well, I am now going to blow my top.

Sally exits L *followed by Peter*

Act II

The Lights fade down L *and fade up* R

The Colonel, in his dressing-gown and carrying earphones, sits at the table, on which rests an air rifle. He reminds one of a naughty boy who has been caught in the act

Sally and Peter enter US

Sally (*as she enters*) Why? I have a right to know. Why?
Colonel According to the terms of the Geneva Convention, a prisoner of war need only give his name, rank and number.
Sally War? What are you talking about? This isn't war.
Colonel It is not my idea of peace, Sally.
Sally I am not leaving until you tell me.
Colonel I am not permitted to tell you.
Sally Why is that?
Colonel I once signed the Official Secrets Act.
Sally I want to know. Tell me. Why did you do it?
Colonel Name, rank and number.
Sally (*turning away*) Oh, for God's sake.
Peter All right, when did you do it: a week ago, a month?
Colonel Name, rank and number.
Sally (*turning back to him*) What you did was monstrous.

The Colonel smiles at her

No father in his right mind bugs his son's house.
Colonel (*chuckling*) Perhaps that's it, Sally. I ought to be certified.
Peter You do understand the enormity of what you did?
Colonel It certainly puts Nuremberg in the shade, doesn't it?
Peter Apart from anything else, it was a gross invasion of our privacy.
Sally You should be full of remorse.
Colonel Oh, but I am. For being found out. Some people aren't. They can record all day and never be found out.
Peter (*gazing at his father*) Who can record all day?
Colonel Pop singers.
Peter You said, and never be found out. What did you mean?
Colonel The fact they cannot sing. Peter Dawson could sing. (*Singing*) "On the road to Mandalay".
Peter (*interrupting*) You know we have your voice on tape, don't you? You know we recorded your voice.
Colonel Yes, I do. And I should like an explanation.
Sally That was only done so that Peter could play it back to you in order to jog your memory. There was nothing sinister about it. It certainly didn't give you the right to eavesdrop on us. What you did was unforgivable. Well, I don't want you in my house ever again. And from now on, you cook for yourself.
Colonel At least I shan't be poisoned.
Sally Poisoned. Who's going to poison you?
Colonel You. Your frozen cannelloni has the consistency of wallpaper paste.

Sally I only wish I had a plate of it in my hand, Dad. You would get it full in the chops.

The Colonel chuckles

I am not putting up with any more rudeness from you.
Colonel Is that why you are off to Bermuda? You need money to make money, Peter. Especially a million. Where did it all come from?
Peter This is typical of you. All innuendo, and nothing to back it up.
Colonel Your ex-wife Judith didn't like the way you did business. She told me. It frightened her.
Peter If you think I'm involved in something crooked, get on to the police.
Colonel I only know the Military Police. I never called them in. That would have been tantamount to failure. I was always able to keep the crime in the family.
Peter Just what is it I'm guilty of?
Colonel The platoon, the company, the regiment. That sort of family. I know no other.
Sally (*staring at him*) You are sick, Dad.
Colonel I had a phone call from Mrs Pearson. She is sick. Caught a bug. (*Chuckling*) As you did.
Sally He thinks it's bloody funny.
Colonel (*no longer chuckling*) Bloody funny! She said she was grateful to you, Peter, for relieving her of all her financial worries. As long as worry is all you relieve her of. Otherwise, if you have a choice, choose the wrath of God.

He notices Sally reach out to touch the rifle

(*Sharply*) Don't touch that air rifle. Don't touch it.
Sally (*moving away*) I wouldn't dare. I don't want my head blown off again. (*Turning on him*) It is so one-sided. All you do is take from us, and all we get in return are threats and criticism. Cook a meal for you and we're trying to poison you.
Colonel I thank you after every meal.
Sally Is that what you mumble to me? I thought it was an apology, in case you couldn't get to the bathroom in time to throw up. You think you're so big, so important. Well, the truth is, Dad, you are a very little man. And what there is, is full of hate.

She turns and stalks out US

Colonel You've landed on your feet with that one, Peter. Why, I think she would even commit murder for you, I told Mabel that. Know what she said? "Well, that's love for you." And laughed. She thought I was joking.
Peter It's like watching a lizard. Out comes the tongue, and another fly disappears. (*He turns to exit*)
Colonel (*leaning across to pick up the air rifle*) Peter.

Peter turns

I meant what I said. The wrath of God would be preferable.

Act II

Peter (*evenly*) Never point a gun at anyone unless you intend to use it.
Colonel Good lad. That's right.
Peter Even if it's unloaded.
Colonel But it isn't unloaded, Peter.

He points it to the ceiling and fires. A light bulb smashes to pieces and there is a Black-out R. *The Colonel chuckles. There is a short silence before Peter speaks*

Peter (*quietly*) Please don't do that in front of Sally, Dad.
Colonel Give her an attack of the vapours, would it?
Peter She is expecting a baby.

There is another short silence as the Colonel exits

Peter wanders over L

The Lights fade up. Sally is already on stage and is still feeling aggrieved whereas Peter is relaxed

(*Chuckling*) You have to admire his cheek. Drilling a hole through brickwork, inserting the mike, running the wires back to his cottage. He must have thought he was fighting the Second World War again. He would have liked that.
Sally We don't happen to be Japanese, Peter.
Peter Such a lot of effort, and all of it wasted. He heard nothing of any consequence. I am on a winning streak, Sally.
Sally I am not having him back in this house.
Peter Not even for his birthday?
Sally When is his birthday?
Peter On Saturday.
Sally Thank you. I shall make sure I have a prior engagement.
Peter (*crossing to put his arms round her*) Sally, we are going to be worth over a million pounds. Knowing that, doesn't the bugging of a room pale into insignificance? Is it worth getting into a tizz about? Be honest. Is it?
Sally (*softening*) No, I suppose not. After all, it could have been worse. He could have bugged our bedroom. My God, that would have sent his heart into overdrive.

They laugh and kiss. Peter then caresses her neck with both hands

Peter Oh, the beautiful white neck of the swan. No wonder it has Royal protection. It is so vulnerable. (*His hands tighten their grip*)
Sally (*quietly*) You are hurting me, Peter.
Peter Only because I love you.

Sally places her hands inside his and pushes against his wrists. He immediately releases his grip and Sally touches her neck

Sally That is the second time you've done that. Don't do it again. I don't like it.
Peter (*smiling*) I'm not the only one who can't control the passion of the moment.
Sally Why, what have I done to you?

Peter I have a bite mark of yours, darling, that would be the envy of Dracula.

Sally gazes at him and then smiles her forgiveness

Sally That wasn't Dracula, that was little Cupid. And if we're not careful, he'll turn us into a couple of mangled wrecks.

And with their arms by their sides they allow their lips to meet. The telephone rings and Peter breaks away to answer it

Know what our last dying words will be? Stop it: I love it.
Peter (*into the receiver*) Yes? ... (*Frowning*) What does that mean? (*Pause*) But you said it was all-systems-go. (*Pause*) You should have warned me. (*Pause*) You never said there might be an objection. ... (*Irritably*) All right, all right, all right; what happens now? ... Nothing? What do you mean, nothing? We offload the shares. (*Pause*) Why not? (*Pause*) But I need the capital. I have to have the capital. ... (*Starting to become angry*) I was not greedy. Now, don't you start blaming me. ... Will you listen? ... Hallo? (*He replaces the receiver*)
Sally Christ, don't tell me it's already turning sour.
Peter Sour? It is rancid. The maggots are on the move.
Sally Why, what has happened?
Peter They said it was foolproof, they said nothing could go wrong.
Sally So what is it that has gone wrong?
Peter Aren't I going to be allowed any peace in this bloody world?
Sally What did you hear?
Peter You can't tell a man he's a millionaire one minute, and then put a bullet in him the next. It is not fair!
Sally What exactly was said just now, Peter? I have a right to know.
Peter (*sitting and endeavouring to compose his thoughts*) Two or three councillors are furious Independent Construction got the tender. They maintain there was an unacceptable level of share-dealing before the announcement.
Sally How do they know?
Peter They had someone monitoring it all.
Sally So what are they after?
Peter An enquiry.
Sally And if that happens?
Peter Independent Construction will lose the tender, shares will plummet, and I will go to prison because I haven't the money to repay my clients.
Sally What's to prevent you from selling all your shares tomorrow?
Peter The syndicate, you stupid woman. I am not a free agent. Besides, get rid of the shares now and that would prove we had prior knowledge that the tender was to go to Independent Construction. That would mean prison for everyone. But leave the shares where they are, and it can all be put down to coincidence. And no-one will go to prison.
Sally Except you.
Peter Because I was a very naughty little boy. I borrowed from my clients

Act II

without their knowledge, without their approval; and little boys don't come naughtier.

Sally You only did it because you were after more income for your clients. And because you were told you couldn't lose.

Peter That is true.

Sally You're too trusting, Peter.

Peter That is also true.

Sally OK. Now, how much do you need before you're in the clear?

Peter Half a million.

Sally (*surprised*) Half a million. As much as that?

Peter Yes, as much as that. I said I was going for the jackpot. Why the surprise?

Sally No-one is going to lend you that kind of money.

Peter I know that.

Sally I shall have to sell the house.

Peter We are not finishing up in slumland, Sally.

Sally You would rather go to prison?

Peter If that is the only alternative, yes.

Sally You are being stupid. I gave you the cottage to sell. Why can't I give you the house?

Peter It is your inheritance. I advised you to buy it.

Sally And very good advice it was too. You will make a healthy profit.

Peter It's your house, it will remain your house. You are not selling it.

Sally Just why are you being so selfish? Because, quite frankly, it's beginning to annoy me.

Peter (*bewildered*) I beg your pardon?

Sally Why can't I have what I want for a change? Why does it always have to be what you want, what you decide?

Peter So what do you want?

Sally I want to sell the house, live in a slum, and be a martyr.

Peter (*smiling*) You are a fool.

Sally (*smiling*) Of course I am. I married you.

Peter You would be prepared to wave goodbye to the new swimming pool, the new extension?

Sally To hell with all that. My God, I am in love, Peter. I shall put the house on the market tomorrow.

Peter Property is sticking. For a quick sale you'll have to drop to three hundred, three hundred and twenty thousand.

Sally So I'll try to borrow the rest.

Peter A waste of time.

Sally You don't know.

Peter Borrowing is something I do know about, Sally. I have made a career of it.

Sally But it's the only way out.

Peter No, it's not.

Sally OK, tell me another way.

Peter There is dear old Dad.

Sally What about dear old Dad?

Peter He could drop down dead at any time. He may already have done so. If not, why not?

Sally stares at him

He is the answer, Sally: the final solution. I mean it. He has to go.
Sally You are not in a rational frame of mind, Peter.
Peter I was when I decided that if the maggots ever started to crawl, he would have to be sacrificed.
Sally No.
Peter He hates us, Sally.
Sally That is not a crime, punishable by death.
Peter He has reached his three score years and ten.
Sally There is no law as yet against living on borrowed time.
Peter He is in poor health. He has a dicky heart.
Sally He will probably get the Queen's telegram.
Peter He believes in euthanasia. He doesn't want to linger. He'd rather be snuffed out like a candle. His own words.
Sally He is not in pain.
Peter He was a professional soldier: kill or be killed his motto.
Sally You are not the enemy.
Peter I have news for you, darling. Anyway, what good is he doing staying alive?
Sally You are not God.
Peter I don't intend to go to prison, Sally.
Sally But that's exactly where you'll end up.
Peter Not if I have a plan.
Sally (*taking a deep breath*) All right. Let us sit down, you and me, and work out a plan. Or would you rather play Scrabble?
Peter (*slowly rising*) Of course. That's what it has to be. Why didn't I think of it before. It's so obvious. (*Looking at Sally*) Can you guess?
Sally The joke has gone on long enough: drop it.
Peter A heart attack. I bring on a heart attack.
Sally (*losing her patience*) He's hardly going to go jogging with you, is he?
Peter A sudden shock could do it. (*Glancing around before gazing at the stairs*) The stairs. Top of the stairs: where the carpet is coming away. I trip. I grab hold of him as I would a lifeline. We fall all the way down. I finish up on top of him. And I stay on top of him. Not for long. Just long enough.
Sally If I thought for a moment you meant it, I would shop you here and now.
Peter Ah, but that is before the event, Sally. Would you shop me after the event?
Sally Yes!
Peter No, give it a little thought. You're in love. You hate it if I have to spend a night away. And it's not as if shopping me will bring him back. Could you do it?
Sally Yes.
Peter I can't believe that. Come on. It's not true, is it?

Act II

Sally I don't know. Probably not. I would probably just walk out of here and fall under a train. God, you've got me so bloody worried, Peter.
Peter Why? I was only testing your loyalty.
Sally Balls.
Peter It was all hypothetical, Sally. I could never do it. I'm far too squeamish. (*Cheerfully*) Do you know, I suddenly feel optimistic. Perhaps there won't be an enquiry. Perhaps, like me, it was all talk. We could make a million yet, Sally. One million pounds: and counting. Can you see them?
Sally (*as she rises and crosses to exit*) All I can see are maggots.

She exits L

Peter (*as he watches her exit*) You won't see any maggots when we arrive back from that world cruise and glide home in the Rolls. No, ma'am. (*Turning, he wanders over to the foot of the stairs and thoughtfully gazes up*)

The Lights fade up to day. It is almost a week later

The Colonel appears from L *and stands looking at Peter*

Peter is edgy, the Colonel wary

Colonel The quack thinks I shouldn't be driving.
Peter He's right. I've never known anyone hog the centre of the road as you do. (*He moves away from the stairs*)
Colonel At least I don't get into the car and pretend I'm driving a Formula Two.
Peter No, you drive as if you're following a hearse.
Colonel As long as I'm following it, and not in it.
Peter Why did the doctor say that to you?
Colonel Something to do with my balance.
Peter (*glancing across*) Your balance?
Colonel Yes, he has changed my pills.
Peter You mean you keep falling over?
Colonel No, it's not a physical thing.
Peter (*losing interest*) Oh.
Colonel He said the pills may make me depressed. But he had already made me depressed when he said "and no alcohol".

As Peter finds it difficult to settle ...

I presume Sally has forgiven me for bugging this room.
Peter You've only been allowed out on parole.
Colonel I've been talking to my accountant about the forthcoming event. When is it due?
Peter When is what due?
Colonel The infant birth.
Peter Why?
Colonel I want it to have some of the money I leave. But I don't want to do it through a trust fund. Too many strangers get too big a percentage. And yet I don't want it to get hold of a large capital sum early in life. It could

ruin the child. The accountant suggested I willed it to Sally and let her follow her maternal instincts in the matter.
Peter You can forget it.
Colonel Oh, I knew you wouldn't much care for that suggestion.
Peter You can forget it because it was a false alarm. She's not expecting. (*He starts to wander again*)
Colonel (*nodding*) Ah. Why are you on edge, Peter. Have you something on your mind?
Peter Yes. Staff problems.
Colonel Not Independent Construction?
Peter Why should Independent Construction concern me?
Colonel Your councillor friend is involved, and there's to be an enquiry.
Peter So I believe.
Colonel Sounds very murky waters to me. One can almost hear the water lapping against the driftwood. And on to the scum.

Sally enters from L carrying a tray on which are crockery, teapot and a round cake

Hallo, no champagne?
Peter You were told no alcohol.
Colonel You didn't know that until just now.
Peter Oh, don't be so bloody childish.
Sally I'm afraid I haven't any candles. (*Putting down the tray*) We'll just have to pretend. (*She prepares to cut the cake*)
Colonel Well, come on. Let's hear from the pair of you.
Peter I beg your pardon?
Colonel (*sitting*) It's my birthday. Aren't you going to sing "Happy Birthday"? And I'm not being childish: I promise.

Sally and Peter glance at each other and then rather self-consciously sing "Happy Birthday"

(*Smiling and meaning it*) Thank you. I enjoyed that. Yes, I did.

The telephone rings three times before Peter can pick up the receiver. He then replaces it

Sally Nobody there?
Peter No, he had already hung up.
Sally (*unconcerned as she cuts the cake*) That's not the first time it has happened. I wonder if it's the same person?
Peter Perhaps it's a heavy breather, who hasn't quite got his act together.
Sally Very odd.
Colonel Yes, very odd, Sally. Thank you both again for the birthday bottle of port. It had better remain in your cellar until I am given the all-clear by the quack.
Peter (*sitting*) It is for laying down.
Colonel I know. A most imaginative present to give to a man of seventy-three.
Peter It need only be for a few years.

Act II

Colonel A few days may be too late, Peter.
Sally (*sharply as she glances across*) Why do you say that?
Colonel Travelling can be hazardous.
Peter Travelling?
Colonel We are off to Italy.

Sally crosses to the Colonel with a slice of cake as Peter rises to gaze at his father

Sally Dad, I'm delighted to hear it. You said "we". Does that mean you're going with a friend?
Colonel My one friend. Mabel Pearson. I telephoned her, said it was time I had a holiday. She asked if she could join me.
Peter When was all this decided?
Colonel When I heard about the enquiry into Independent Construction. I said to myself: Percy, I think it's time you picked up your bed and walked.

Sally offers Peter a slice of cake, but he waves it away

Peter How long are you going for?
Colonel A month.
Peter When are you going?
Colonel Thursday. But I am staying at the village hotel as from this evening. I feel in the mood for company. There are times when one can be too lonely.
Sally Italy can be very romantic.
Colonel Strange you should say that. I should like to have shared a room with Mabel.
Sally (*startled*) You. Share a room?
Colonel Have I shocked you?
Sally No. Well, yes. But not in the way you think.
Peter My God. Mother hasn't been dead a year, and here you are wanting to hop into bed with another woman.
Colonel Your wife wasn't even dead when you climbed into bed with Sally. All I want is a little warmth. That is all.
Peter (*gazing across at the stairs*) Do you love this Pearson woman?
Colonel Oh, it's this Pearson woman now.
Peter Do you?
Colonel What is love? Fondness; friendship; laughter? Then, yes. Depends on your definition.
Sally You are a sentimentalist, Dad.
Colonel Yes, I am a sentimentalist. I loved the Music Hall for that reason. When the top of the bill sang, he or she always finished with a song, I would feel the tears coming. (*He sings a snatch of "The Boy I Love is Up in the Gallery"*)
Peter (*interrupting*) Except it's all surface with a sentimentalist, isn't it? There's no depth.
Colonel In my Army days, Sally, there was always the barrack-room lawyer. Now I suppose he has to contend with the barrack-room psychologist. "Why is Nobby always bursting into tears, Shorty? I mean,

he has only lost an arm and a leg." "I will tell you, Spike. He's a sentimentalist. No depth."
Sally (*laughing*) You asked for that, Peter.
Colonel (*glancing at his watch*) I mustn't forget to take my pills.
Peter (*coldly*) Yes, you make sure you stay alive.
Colonel I shall.
Peter And hold on to all that money of yours. Why, live another twenty years, and it may be just enough to bury you.
Colonel I may bury you first.
Peter It's possible. You buried Simon.

The Colonel gazes at him

He didn't want to go into the Army.
Sally Do you, er, do you hope to visit Florence, Dad?

The Colonel holds his gaze for a moment before transferring it to Sally

Colonel I'm quite sure Mabel will want to write her postcards from there. (*With an affectionate smile*) She likes people to know she is cultural.
Sally Do you intend to get married?
Colonel Peter said something to her, because I am now a geriatric in her eyes. In fact, she's probably wondering how she's going to get the corpse back to England. But here is the irony, Sally. We would not have married. Simply lived together, that's what senior citizens do nowadays. Their respective offspring prefer it that way. You see, wills need never be touched. What was coming to the little darlings will still come to them. So you needn't have worried, Peter.
Peter I was not worried.
Colonel You are now. You took a million-pound gamble: and you lost. Did you steal from your clients?
Peter Mrs Pearson's capital is safe. I can do nothing without her authorization.
Colonel I thought she gave you *carte blanche*.
Peter I have a photostat of the agreement upstairs. Do you want to see it?
Colonel Yes, I do.
Peter Then if you will kindly follow me.
Sally (*sharply*) He doesn't have to go with you. You can bring it down to him.

Peter waits until he has reached the foot of the stairs before turning

Peter I thought Dad might also like to see the alterations we have in mind.
Colonel Alterations?
Peter Yes, on two floors. Upstairs is to be a conservatory and have a glass dome. It will mean going out about twenty feet.
Colonel (*frowning*) Twenty feet? But that would destroy my view of the trees.
Peter I don't think so.
Colonel Of course it would.
Peter Come and have a look, the plans are on our bed.

Act II

Colonel (*as he exits*) I am not having my view destroyed.

The Colonel exits upstairs

Sally I told you I want to sell the house, Peter.
Peter I only want to get him going, Sally. He is becoming too cocky.
Sally You said it was all hypothetical.
Peter Nothing is going to happen. I give you my word.

He exits upstairs

Sally watches him exit. She glances at the stairs as she starts to collect the tea-things

Colonel (*off; his voice raised in anger*) You'll never get planning permission for this.
Peter (*off*) I do have friends on the council, Dad.
Colonel (*off*) You are doing it deliberately. You know how much I love those trees. I will not allow it.
Peter (*off*) Calm down, or you'll have a seizure.

Sally crosses to the stairs and starts to climb

Colonel (*off*) You have made me so angry. You never told me you were planning an extension when you sold me the cottage. It will look hideous!

The Colonel appears at the top of the stairs and starts to descend

Do you want to turn the village into a cesspit?

Peter quickly appears

He crashes against the Colonel, who stumbles, but is saved from falling by Sally's body. Unable to regain his balance, Peter falls to the foot of the stairs and lies there. Sally looks at a very shaken Colonel before going to Peter's assistance. Peter sits up

Sally What did you come charging down like that for? You knew the carpet was loose.
Peter (*gazing at her*) You bloody bitch.
Sally It was your fault. You tripped on the loose carpet. I said there would be an accident one day.

As Peter gets to his feet and walks away...

Thank God no-one was hurt.

She turns to the Colonel, who is holding on to the rail

You'd better come and sit down, Dad.
Colonel (*remaining motionless*) Keep away from me.
Sally (*starting to climb*) I'll give you an arm, and you can lean against me.
Colonel I said keep away.

Sally gazes at him and then retraces her steps

Sally The men in this house are always so grateful.

Peter It was lucky you were on the stairs, Sally.
Sally Thank you. Yes, it was.
Colonel It's cover-up time now, is it? A moment ago she was a bloody bitch. Your co-ordination was abysmal.
Sally If I hadn't been on the stairs, you could have had a nasty fall.
Colonel But that was the plan. For me to have a nasty fall.
Sally It was an accident.
Colonel It was attempted murder. And we all know why it was done, so let us forgo the euphemisms, please. How were you going to finish me off: or were you hoping the shock would do it? When is the next attempt to be? Remember, you only have until this evening. I should do it now. Get it over with. Turn on the charm again, Sally, so that Peter can catch me off guard.
Sally You are being silly, Dad.
Colonel I bug this room, and that was monstrous. You two try to murder me, and I am being silly.
Sally We did not try to murder you.
Colonel How much did you steal, Peter?
Peter (*sitting*) I did not steal. I borrowed.
Colonel How much?
Peter Four hundred thousand.
Colonel (*staring*) Four hundred thousand?
Peter Give or take the odd fifty p.
Colonel (*slowly crossing to Peter*) Who from?
Peter I was able to get a loan.
Colonel Not for the full amount. Where did the rest come from? From the likes of Mabel Pearson? Did you steal from Mabel Pearson?
Peter I borrowed a few grand from her account, yes.
Colonel I knew it.
Peter I shall pay it back. All I need is time.
Colonel What, so that you can steal from some other gullible old lady?
Peter Perhaps Mrs Pearson shouldn't have been so gullible.

The Colonel lifts his hand as if to strike Peter across the face

Peter (*tensing and half-rising*) Don't push your luck, old man: OK?
Colonel (*stabbing a finger at him*) Or you, Peter. Or you. Now, you said you'd pay it back. How? I want to know how.
Peter (*relaxing*) You could always lend me the money. Sell your shares. Sell the cottage. Move in with us. You're better off than most. You have your Army pension. Index-linked.

The Colonel continues to gaze at him

I'm not very good at pleading.
Colonel No, you are not.
Peter I would appreciate some help. If only to pay Mrs Pearson her monthly income.
Colonel If I'm going to help you, I shall want to know the truth. Not in dribs and drabs. All of it. Now.

Act II

Peter I borrowed more than a few grand from Mrs Pearson. And from the others.
Colonel How much more?
Peter The lot.
Colonel The lot? You could do that to people who trusted you, who had faith in you? My God, out of the millions of sperm you had to be the one.
Sally He was told it was foolproof. If it had come off, his clients would have made a hundred per cent on their capital.
Colonel Trash.
Sally That is why Peter did it.
Colonel More trash. (*To Peter*) How much did you borrow on the house?
Peter I didn't.
Colonel Why didn't you?
Peter To begin with, it's Sally's house. She owns it.
Colonel (*turning to stare at Sally*) You used other people's money, but not your own?
Sally I can explain.
Colonel What is there to explain? You refused to raise a loan on the house.
Sally I did not refuse.
Colonel You were not going to lose out, were you?
Sally I promise you I was prepared to ——
Colonel (*interrupting*) If you thought the scheme was foolproof, why did you leave yourself a financial bolt-hole?
Sally I agreed with Peter that it would be ——
Colonel (*interrupting*) Of course you did. You were his partner. You condoned everything he did.
Sally No.
Colonel I have your voice on tape. You said the news was better than an orgasm.

Alarmed by his expression, Sally backs away

You said I was not safe from a grizzly end. You wondered how you would do it.
Sally That is not true.
Colonel I have it on tape: it is all on tape!
Peter Tell me, is it suicide if you bring on your own heart attack?
Colonel (*less angry as he turns to Peter*) You asked for help. It will take me some time to work out the details. Be in my cottage at twenty hundred hours. Bring that whore with you.

The Colonel exits L

There is a short silence

Sally (*quietly*) I now know how someone like me could murder an old man.

Peter glances across at her

And it is very frightening...

The telephone rings three times before stopping, and the Lights slowly fade

There is darkness for a moment or two before the Lights fade up R. *It is eight o'clock the same night*

The Colonel pushes the table (on which there is a pistol in its holster) upstage and then conceals the gun and holster on the dresser DR. *He then arranges three chairs, picks up the shotgun, sits, places the gun on his lap, the barrel pointing away from the other two chairs and becomes motionless*

There is a knock at the door

Colonel Enter.

Peter and Sally enter

Sit down.
Sally (*staring at the gun*) Why the shotgun?
Colonel People keep reminding me that I am an old man. Well, old men sometimes need help to defend themselves.
Sally I am not staying unless you get rid of that shotgun.
Colonel You are in no position to dictate terms. Sit down.
Peter (*sitting*) He said he would help us. Do as you're told: sit down.

Sally sits

Have you been able to work out the details, Dad?
Colonel Yes, I have.
Peter What are they? We'll agree to anything.
Colonel Sally will transfer the deeds of your house to me.
Peter (*frowning*) But surely that's unnecessary. She can raise a loan on it herself.
Colonel The moment it is legally binding I shall return the tape. I shall then sell the house and all its contents, plus your cars. The money to be divided among Mrs Pearson and your other clients.
Peter Go to hell. This isn't going to be the pound of flesh, is it? This is going to be the body and blood.
Sally It won't be enough to save Peter. He will still go to prison.
Colonel No, because he will sell his practice.
Peter Sell my practice?
Colonel Yes. You are guilty of gross professional misconduct, and you will retire.
Peter But if I give you my word that from now on ——
Colonel (*interrupting*) Your word, Peter? Your word is worth less than your own vomit. You will grant my solicitor Power of Attorney. He will get the best price he can.
Peter You don't intend to help me at all, do you?
Colonel If there is still a deficit, I shall make up the shortfall by selling some of my own personal investments.
Peter But surely you can leave me with something.
Colonel You have your health.
Sally And a loving wife.
Colonel You think your marriage will survive this?

Act II

Sally Yes, because it is beyond your jurisdiction. Tell me, would you be prepared to give Peter a loan, so that he could start a little business somewhere?
Colonel No, I would not.
Sally You don't believe in the quality of mercy?
Colonel I believe in an eye for an eye. He would have left Mabel to starve.
Sally But she wouldn't have starved. She had you. Well, Peter has got me.
Colonel You have no money.
Sally I would break rocks for your son.
Colonel (*holding his gaze for a moment before glancing at Peter*) Oh, I almost forgot. There is a codicil. You'll get nothing from me when I die. I shall attend to that tomorrow.

Peter springs at him, not caring what happens. The Colonel brings up the gun in order to parry the expected blow. Peter grabs the gun with both hands. There is a short trial of strength. Peter wins and points the barrel at the Colonel, who slowly rises

Sally (*shouting*) Don't Peter! For God's sake, don't, Peter!

Peter stares at his father. He continues to stare as he backs and hands the gun to Sally.

Peter You do it, Sally.
Sally No.
Peter Think of the way he has treated you. Kill him.
Sally No.
Peter We can easily make it appear like suicide.
Sally No!
Colonel (*realizing the danger is over and sitting*) I have to say I am relieved to find your love for my son does have its limitations, Sally.
Sally (*placing the gun on the table*) I didn't promise to obey him, merely to cherish him.
Colonel You can cherish a man who orders you to kill?
Sally That just shows the emotional state you've got him into.
Colonel But was he in such an emotional state? Or was he quietly working out his future? I mean, if it is that easy to turn murder into suicide, why didn't he press the trigger? Why did he want you to do it?
Sally Destroying my love for him would be the *coup de grâce*, wouldn't it, Dad?
Colonel Not at all.
Sally Good. I should hate to disappoint you.
Colonel I've arranged for you to see my solicitor at three o'clock tomorrow. Be sure to bring the deeds of the house with you.
Peter What did you tell him?
Colonel I said you were emigrating.
Peter Emigrating. Why?
Colonel I should have thought it was obvious.
Peter Tell me.
Colonel To save your hide.

Peter That can't possibly be the reason. You don't give a damn about me: never have done. It's your pride, isn't it; your stupid bloody pride. You don't want people to think you might have failed as a father. Yes, well, I don't know that I want to be sentenced by your court martial. Why shouldn't I have a proper trial?

Colonel You would still be found guilty.

Peter Thank you, but if you don't mind, we'll leave that to a proper judge and jury. You'll be a witness, Dad. You will be able to stand in the box and tell the court you are worth nearly half a million pounds. And, no, you didn't lend your son a penny of it. You'll be able to say his word is worth less than his own vomit. No doubt about it, Dad. You'll get the sympathy of the court straight away. You'll be able to compare me with my brother.

Colonel (*frowning*) You cannot drag him in.

Peter Oh, yes, I can: and, oh, yes, I will.

Colonel The man is dead.

Peter Is he really? Now, that is news to me. Is that news to you, Sally?

Colonel You will not mention his name.

Peter Mother, God rest her soul, should be good for a morning.

Colonel Your mother?

Peter And Mrs Pearson for another morning.

Colonel (*bewildered*) No, this is inadmissible.

Peter The judge will decide that, Dad. He may decide it is. Or he may decide it's not. All I know is, once a court is in session the dirt flies and the mud sticks. And I shan't be squeamish about defending myself. It will be an eye for an eye. I learned that from my daddy.

Colonel (*after a short silence*) In that case, Sally will also have to stand trial.

Sally (*evenly*) Why? I am willing to give you the deeds of the house. But not if I have to stand trial.

Colonel You are equally guilty.

Sally And you are being stupid. If I get off, which I will, I keep the house. And Mrs Pearson will get nothing.

Colonel (*to Sally*) You would hand over the deeds of the house?

Sally And the contents. But only to save Peter from prison.

Peter No, to hell with it. We shall both stand trial. I look forward to seeing Mrs Pearson's expression when she hears the news.

Colonel What news?

Peter That Sally was perfectly willing to sell the house, plus everything else, and give the proceeds to Mrs Pearson and the others. But you spurned the offer. You insisted the law must take its course. And the result? Sally goes free, and Mrs Pearson starts queueing at Social Security. Now that has to be a human interest story worth following up. The tabloids will have a field day. "Wealthy Lover Snees At Poor Widow's Plight". "Army Rat Leaves Mabel To Starve". It is decision time for you, old man. What do you intend to do?

Colonel You cannot keep getting away with it, Peter.

Peter Then start the ball rolling. Go to the police.

Colonel I am prepared to compromise.

Peter This is not an armistice, Dad. This is unconditional surrender. You either agree with my terms, or you don't. Which is it to be? Just look at him. Strip him of his power, and what is left? Nothing but the death-rattle. And to think he could once put the fear of God into me. You were a tyrant, Papa.

Colonel Why? Because I tried to discipline you? Because I tried to stop you getting away with murder? Strange that. You've always tried to get away with murder.

Peter You gave me a hell of a time. I shall never forgive you.

Colonel (*with a wry smile*) Like your mother. She never forgave me.

Sally What didn't she forgive you for?

Colonel My one infidelity.

Sally You had an affair?

Colonel It lasted six weeks. Must be twenty-five years ago. Jill and I never made love again. With anyone.

Sally I bet it was Mrs Pearson. Was it, Dad?

No reply

Of course it was. (*Admiringly*) You old devil.

Peter Mabel Pearson was my mother's best friend. There's no excuse for that sort of thing.

Sally You are being pompous, Peter. Twenty-five years without sex. That is a savage sentence. Why, he didn't even get remission for good behaviour. How did you stick it, Dad?

Colonel Duty. It was my duty to stick it.

Sally You're from a vanished age, Colonel. I mean, what was it like at the Battle of Hastings? You must have been there.

Peter Let's get out of this stinking hole.

Colonel Peter, if I make funds available, will you arrange for Mabel Pearson and the others to get their money back? It's very important to me.

Peter It's in my interest that they do.

Colonel Yes, you're right, it is. I'd forgotten that. Then they will. Without a doubt.

Peter Mind you, they may not get it all back. After all, I am entitled to certain expenses.

Colonel No, no. You're entitled to nothing. Because what you did was wrong.

Peter Only if I'm found out. The trick is not to be found out.

Colonel Like wife-bashing?

Sally Wife-bashing? But that is ludicrous.

Colonel Ask the one before you.

Sally Peter has never harmed me.

Colonel You have been lucky.

Peter Save your breath, Dad. It is not going to work.

Colonel You haven't had his hands round your throat.

Sally touches her throat

You haven't lost consciousness, because of his hands round your throat.
Peter Did you ever see bruises on Judith?
Colonel The police saw bruises.
Peter They were self-inflicted.
Colonel The police didn't think so. Fortunately for Peter, she retracted her statement, and no charges were brought.
Peter And shortly after that she volunteered to see a psychiatrist, so stop twisting things.
Colonel Who persuaded her to volunteer?
Peter Old men do like to rabbit on, don't they? Now, either you agree to my terms, or Sally and I both stand trial.
Sally What are the terms?
Peter He gives me everything he owns, including the cottage.
Sally No, I'm not having that. You're just being vindictive.
Peter (*to his father*) I shall let you sleep on it. No, I shan't. Be in my house at twenty-three hundred hours.
Colonel No, wait. I have something for you. I came across this the other day. It belonged to Simon. It is still in working order. (*He picks up the pistol in its holster*) I held it in reserve. It was to be my second line of defence. But circumstances have changed. I am now going on to the offensive.
Peter Would you have put Simon through this?
Colonel I may not have understood your brother either, had he lived. Your trouble is, Peter, you have lived too long. Why not end it now? Here. Do something worthwhile for once.

He holds out the pistol and holster to Peter who removes the pistol, points it at the Colonel, and then puts it back in the holster

Peter Did you really think I would shoot myself? Are you that senile? Or were you hoping I would shoot you?
Colonel I knew you wouldn't have the guts. You proved that earlier. Pushing someone in the back is one thing. But to blow open a man's head and see the blood spurt out is something else. And one bullet may not have been enough. You may have needed a second. And a third.
Sally Look, I'm sorry, but I've had quite enough of the pair of you and your sadistic pleasures for one night. I'm going to bed.
Colonel No, don't go, Sally. I'm worried about your future. Whether you have one.
Peter You so hate losing, don't you?
Colonel (*sitting*) We are not playing a round of golf, Peter. We are discussing life and death. Sally's life and death.
Peter Sally is living, and will continue to go on living.
Colonel You've nothing to worry about, Sally. As the hangman said to Ruth Ellis. But then you're not entirely safe, are you, Peter? Unlike me, she may spill the beans. And time isn't on your side, because the more one gets to know you, the more repulsive you become. Sally will find that out, just as your first wife did.
Sally What did Judith find out?

Act II

Peter Take no notice of him, Sally.
Sally I want to know what she found out. Tell me.
Colonel Three rings on the telephone means she is waiting.
Peter Trash.
Sally Who is waiting?
Colonel Whoever happens to be the flavour of the month.
Peter More trash.
Colonel His latest peccadillo.
Sally Christ Almighty, the three rings started even before we were married.
Colonel With Judith it started before they were married.
Sally (*her eyes blazing at Peter*) You bastard.
Peter Congratulations, Dad. You were right. She could commit murder. But I didn't realize I was to be the corpse.
Colonel You won't be a corpse, because you cannot swing for it now.
Peter Swing for what?
Colonel Murder. But you can be put away. You ought to be put away. And if Sally believes in justice, you will be put away.
Peter Who am I supposed to have murdered?
Colonel (*keeping a wary eye on Peter and wrapping a handkerchief round the pistol as he withdraws it from the holster*) All I know is the only fingerprints on this weapon are yours, Peter. (*Letting the holster drop to the floor*) I was wrong about you, Sally. Do forgive me. And remember what I said. (*Pointing the pistol at Peter*) You could say this is going to be almost as good as a brainwash. Appeal dismissed. Sentence of this Court Martial to be carried out forthwith. May I be forever in your thoughts, son. (*He suddenly contorts himself and points the barrel at his head. He presses the trigger and slumps dead in the chair*)

Sally and Peter, rooted to the spot, stare at the corpse. After a moment or two, Peter smiles, chuckles and then laughs. Sally turns to look at him and, during Peter's speech, slowly picks up the shotgun. Peter bends down to make sure his father is dead

Peter The King is dead. (*Picking up the pistol, rising and gazing down*) Long live the King. Halleluiah. Do you know, this is the best present you have ever given me, Dad. I have but one little criticism. You should have given it to me earlier. About thirty years earlier. (*He bends down to pick up the handkerchief*)
Sally (*with controlled nervous intensity*) Leave that handkerchief where it is.
Peter (*glancing across to find the shotgun aimed at him*) Why?
Sally I want your fingerprints on that pistol. I want you to be found guilty of murder.
Peter (*straightening up*) You can't mean that, Sally.
Sally (*nodding*) I do.
Peter No. You're hysterical because of what you have just seen. (*Casually turning his back on her*) Don't be taken in by Dad's ravings, Sally. Don't let him come between us. Don't let him win, darling. (*He crouches as he spins round. Holding the pistol, he fires at Sally. But only the click of the trigger is heard. And a second click. And a third. Slowly he straightens up*)

Sally Phone nine nine nine. Get the police over here.
Peter You couldn't fire that thing, Sally.
Sally Oh, yes. But I don't intend to be one of love's little martyrs. If I shoot, it will be in self-defence. I saw you murder your father.
Peter Is that what you're going to tell the police?
Sally Yes.
Peter You haven't the staying power, Sally. If you don't break down before, you will break down in court.
Sally No, because whenever I think of you, I shall hear a ringing in my ears. Three rings each time.
Peter That gun may not be loaded.
Sally Then take a gamble, Peter. You like a gamble. Take it.

Curtain

FURNITURE AND PROPERTY LIST

ACT I

On stage: *Area* L—*living-room*:
Chairs
Drinks table. *On it*: glasses, bottles of drink including gin, brandy, whisky, sherry, Campari, soda, tonic, ice-bucket with ice, table lamp
Hi-fi. *In it*: cassette. *By it*: other cassettes, records
Coffee table
Small table. *On it*: table lamp, telephone
Fireplace. *On wall beside it*: servants' bell
Rugs

Area R—*kitchen*:
Table. *On it*: dead rabbit, shotgun, cleaning cloth, knife
3 chairs
Dresser. *On it*: telephone
Dead hare on hook

Other dressing for both areas as required

Off stage: Suitcase (**Colonel**)
Tray with plate of cheese and biscuits, knife (**Sally**)
Suitcase (**Colonel**)
Car keys (**Mabel**)
Documents (**Peter**)
Briefcase containing papers (**Peter**)

During Black-out on page 21:

   Area L:

Strike: Dirty glasses
Papers, documents, briefcases
Set: Scrabble, pen, paper on coffee table

Personal: **Sally:** wrist-wtch
Peter: wrist-watch   } required throughout
Colonel: wrist-watch

ACT II

Strike: *Area* L:
Scrabble, pen, notepad
Area R:
Rabbit, hare, shotgun, cleaning cloth, knife

Set:	*Area* L: Paperback for **Sally** New fitting on servants' bell, with long thin microphone and flex behind casing
	Area R: Air rifle, earphones on table
Off stage:	Tray with cups, saucers, spoons, plates, pot of tea, jug of milk, knife, cake on plate (**Sally**)

During Black-out on page 42:

Strike:	*Area* B: Air rifle, earphones
Set:	Pistol in holster on table Shotgun
Personal:	**Colonel:** handkerchief, concealed blood sac

LIGHTING PLOT

Practical fittings required: 2 table lamps L, pendant R
2 Interiors: a living-room and a kitchen

ACT I

To open: Evening—general lighting L, table lamps on

Cue 1	**Peter** and **Sally** exit L *Fade to black-out*	(Page)
Cue 2	When ready *Bring up general afternoon lighting R*	(Page)
Cue 3	**Colonel** and **Mabel** exit *Cross-fade to L—evening—general lighting, table lamps on*	(Page 1)
Cue 4	**Colonel** slowly straightens up, puzzled *Fade to black-out*	(Page 2)
Cue 5	When ready *Bring up general lighting L—day*	(Page 2)

ACT II

To open: Night—general lighting L, table lamps on

Cue 6	**Peter** follows **Sally** off L *Cross-fade to R—general lighting, pendant on*	(Page 2)
Cue 7	As **Colonel** fires rifle at light bulb *Black-out R*	(Page 3)
Cue 8	**Peter** wanders over to area L *Fade up general lighting L, table lamps on*	(Page 3)
Cue 9	**Peter** wanders over to foot of stairs and gazes thoughtfully up *Change to day lighting L*	(Page 3)
Cue 10	Telephone rings three times *Slowly fade to black-out*	(Page 4)
Cue 11	When ready *Bring up lighting R—pendant on*	(Page 4)

EFFECTS PLOT

ACT I

Cue 1	**Sally** crosses to hi-fi and presses button	(Page 8)
	Sound of cassette re-winding	
Cue 2	**Sally** presses then play buttons	(Page 8)
	Stop re-wind, then voices of Colonel and Peter as page 9	
Cue 3	**Sally** presses stop button	(Page 9)
	Cut tape	
Cue 4	**Peter:** "...Scrooge Benevolent Society."	(Page 9)
	Telephone rings 3 times	
Cue 5	Shortly after lights come up R	(Page 10)
	Car stops outside, car door opens and closes	
Cue 6	**Mabel:** "...the bridge class——"	(Page 11)
	Car horn off	
Cue 7	**Mabel:** "...I'd be so grateful."	(Page 19)
	Faint alarm bell off	
Cue 8	**Peter** follows **Sally** out	(Page 19)
	Cut alarm bell	
Cue 9	**Mabel** exits; **Colonel** starts to flick through papers	(Page 21)
	Click of cassette stopping, then button popping out	
Cue 10	**Colonel** presses re-wind button	(Page 21)
	Cassette re-winds	
Cue 11	**Colonel** presses stop and play buttons	(Page 21)
	Stop re-wind, then voices of Mabel and Colonel as page 21	
Cue 12	**Colonel** stops cassette and presses wind button	(Page 21)
	Sound of cassette winding—stop after a few moments	
Cue 13	**Colonel:** "Yes."	(Page 22)
	Pause, then click of cassette stopping	
Cue 14	**Sally:** "...not to do it ever again."	(Page 24)
	Telephone rings	

ACT II

Cue 15	Shortly after Act II begins	(Page 27)
	Telephone rings	
Cue 16	**Peter** taps outer casing of servants' bell	(Page 28)
	Static noise	
Cue 17	**Colonel** fires rifle at light bulb	(Page 31)
	Light bulb smashes	

The Last Gamble 53

| Cue 18 | **Sally** and **Peter** kiss
Telephone rings | (Page 32) |
|---|---|---|
| Cue 19 | **Colonel:** "Yes, I did."
Telephone rings 3 times | (Page 36) |
| Cue 20 | **Sally:** "And it is very frightening …"
Telephone rings 3 times | (Page 41) |
| Cue 21 | **Colonel** fires pistol
Pistol shot | (Page 47) |